אֵין כֵּאלֹהֵינוּ

AYN KELOHEYNU

BY NOAH GOLINKIN

**Learn to comprehend the Hebrew
prayerbook in a new way
a sequel to SHALOM ALEICHEM**

SHENGOLD PUBLISHERS

Dedicated to
my friends Sylvia and Alex Hassan
and to
the leaders of the National Federation of Jewish Men's Clubs,
the farsighted sponsors of the Hebrew Literacy Campaign.

Fifth Printing, 1989
ISBN 0-88400-136-9

Library of Congress Catalog Card Number: 81-51960

Published by Shengold Publishers, Inc.
18 West 45th St., New York, N.Y. 10036

Printed in the United States of America

FOREWORD

The National Federation of Jewish Men's Clubs, a synagogue-oriented organization, was deeply concerned with the number of people within our congregations who were unable to read Hebrew. A campaign was undertaken with the goal of eradicating Hebrew illiteracy. We labelled this project "The Hebrew Literacy Campaign." The program attempts to teach Hebrew reading to a maximum number of people in a minimum time. The author, Rabbi Noah Golinkin, employed a unique method designed to teach Hebrew reading skills to the adult community. His first textbook, *Shalom Aleichem,* was focused on the Friday Sabbath Eve Service and was an immediate success. Tens of thousands of adults learned to read Hebrew in crash courses of twelve weekly two-hour sessions taught by lay teachers.

In order to fulfill the needs of those who had learned Hebrew with *Shalom Aleichem* and who wished to become more proficient, the National Federation of Jewish Men's Clubs encouraged Rabbi Golinkin to produce a second work.

Ayn Keloheynu is a lucid, illustrated textbook and workbook for Level II students. Like its predecessor, it employs the "Golinkin Method" of study; however, this book focuses on the liturgy of the Shabbat Morning Service, emphasizing fluency, historical background, contemporary relevance and a thorough understanding of the text. It is indeed a fascinating adventure in the study of Hebrew.

The first edition of this book was so well received that an additional printing was almost immediately planned. This second edition retains most of the original material with some minor corrections and improvements.

With this book, Rabbi Golinkin has made another contribution to Hebrew learning and adult Jewish education. It is our hope that his works, as used in our Hebrew Literacy campaign, will result in a greater participation in Hebrew and in congregational life.

Arthur S. Bruckman
Chairman, Hebrew Literacy Campaign

INTRODUCTION

The book *Ayn Keloheynu* teaches comprehension of eighteen select prayers of the Shabbat Morning Service. The book consists of two parts: one for classroom and one for home and classroom.

It aims at

1) increasing reading fluency,

2) understanding of the underlying ideas of the prayers,

3) learning the rituals of the prayer services,

4) acquiring a limited basic Hebrew vocabulary of the prayerbook, and

5) acquiring a 99-word "Vocabulary of Jewish Life" (words like *Minyan*, *Maftir*, etc.).

The specific methodology for teaching this book is provided in a separate pamphlet containing a comprehensive Teacher's Guide and Syllabus.

The programmed structure of the book, the layout of the prayer-texts and the consistent methodology are aimed at making the book easy to teach and to learn.

The book can be studied as is. However, linguistic interests may differ. For that reason, Part II of the book provides an "Extended Hebrew Vocabulary" for those who wish to study Hebrew vocabulary more intensively. The Guide on the other hand provides guidance as to how those who wish to omit study of Hebrew vocabulary may do so easily.

In order not to overburden the new learner, the *dagesh hazak* is not taught in this book.

Part II of the book also contains the "Vocabulary of Jewish Life," geared primarily at home study.

Due to the unique methodological techniques provided in the Guide a great deal of learning will "happen" in the classroom: overall comprehension of the prayers, vocabulary learning and developing of reading fluency. The classroom discussion of ideas will call forth active student participation and will give the class new vistas of understanding the prayers. The method requires no memorization of Hebrew vocabulary but stresses homework, attendance at services and listening to cassettes of the congregational tunes of your own congregation as essential ingredients of acquiring fluency.

As was the case with the *Shalom Aleichem* book the teaching of *Ayn Keloheynu* will hopefully turn out to be an easily manageable and highly rewarding experience to the volunteer lay teachers, and it will give the learners a sense of continuous progress and cumulative achievement.

We hope that *Ayn Keloheynu* will add significant meaning to the lives of teachers and learners alike and will help create a new enthusiasm in the lives of Jewish congregations everywhere.

Tishrei, 5742
October, 1981

Noah Golinkin

ACKNOWLEDGMENTS

I wish to extend my deep appreciation to one of the educational mentors of our time, Dr. Louis Kaplan, President Emeritus of Baltimore Hebrew College, for his wise counsel on the overall direction of the book.

I am immensely grateful to Rabbi David Blumenfeld, Director of the National Federation of Jewish Men's Clubs, Rabbi Yaakov Rosenberg, Vice Chancellor of the Jewish Theological Seminary, Rabbi Matthew Clark, Director of the Board of Jewish Education of Greater Washington, Mr. Ari West, Educational Consultant of the Board of Jewish Education of Greater Washington, Rabbi Leonard Cahan and Mrs. Elizabeth Cahan, Har Shalom Congregation, Potomac, Maryland, and Rabbi David Golinkin, instructor in Talmud and Rabbinics, Jewish Theological Seminary, for their thorough review and constructive critique of the manuscript.

My sincere thanks to Hadassah Blocker, chairperson of Adult Education, New England Branch of Women's League for Conservative Judaism, Rachel Ginsburg of Bethpage Jewish Community Center, my student Sandy Bender, and Cantor Abraham Golinkin of Adas Israel Congregation, Washington, D.C., for their significant insights and classroom feedback.

I am deeply indebted to the noted sculptor Nathan Rapoport for his graciousness in allowing me to include his work "The memorial in memory of the Jewish children who perished in the Holocaust, New York" in this book.

My appreciation to Dr. and Mrs. Julius Siegel and to my students, Aylene Kovensky, Becky Lessey and Bill Lieber, for their valuable editorial and technical assistance.

I thank all the artists whose works beautify the book. A special thanks to the nationally renowned artist Phillip Ratner for the "Kadosh" specially created for this book; to Shai Zauderer for his skillfulness and unstinting effort in preparing the art and design of the book; and to the late Margaret Yane for many of her sketches.

I am most grateful to my publisher, Moshe A. Sheinbaum, for his constant encouragement, his stimulating ideas and painstaking care in publishing this book.

And finally, my deepest gratitude to my wife, Dvorah, for her patience, understanding and involvement.

THE AUTHOR

TABLE OF CONTENTS

Part I (for classroom)

Part II (for home and classroom)

אֵין כֵּאלֹהֵינוּ

AN INVITATION

We invite you to join us
on a voyage of discovery.
We shall be searching —
for the meaning of words
and the meaning behind the words;
for the message of the prayers
and the story behind the prayers;
for the standard formulas of some prayers
and for the hidden structures of others.

Our book begins at a point where
the Saturday and Holiday services end:
with אֵין כֵּאלֹהֵינוּ.
Religious Jewish experience is not linear.
It is an ongoing cycle; end and beginning meet.
Interestingly enough,
one of the first religious words a very young Jewish child learns
is the word that comes at the end of every blessing:

אֵין כֵּאלֹהֵינוּ (on p... of your prayerbook)

אֵין כֵּאלֹהֵינוּ makes an important statement of Jewish belief.
In addition it also carries a hidden statement of Jewish prayer methodology.
We shall try to unfold this hidden statement step by step.
Each line below carries a full stanza. Each stanza consists of 4 phrases (a, b, c, d) of 2 or 3 words.
As we unravel the message of each stanza we shall discover the "code" which governs the sequence of the stanzas.

(d)		(c)		(b)		(a)	
כְּמוֹשִׁיעֵנוּ	אֵין	כְּמַלְכֵּנוּ	אֵין	כַּאדוֹנֵינוּ	אֵין	כֵּאלֹהֵינוּ	אֵין
כְּמוֹשִׁיעֵנוּ	מִי	כְּמַלְכֵּנוּ	מִי	כַּאדוֹנֵינוּ	מִי	כֵּאלֹהֵינוּ	מִי
לְמוֹשִׁיעֵנוּ	נוֹדֶה	לְמַלְכֵּנוּ	נוֹדֶה	לַאדוֹנֵינוּ	נוֹדֶה	לֵאלֹהֵינוּ	נוֹדֶה
מוֹשִׁיעֵנוּ	בָּרוּךְ	מַלְכֵּנוּ	בָּרוּךְ	אֲדוֹנֵינוּ	בָּרוּךְ	אֱלֹהֵינוּ	בָּרוּךְ
מוֹשִׁיעֵנוּ	אַתָּה הוּא	מַלְכֵּנוּ	אַתָּה הוּא	אֲדוֹנֵינוּ	אַתָּה הוּא	אֱלֹהֵינוּ	אַתָּה הוּא

(handwritten notes beside table a: "there is none", "who", "let us give thanks", "blessed be", "You are he")

	(d)	(c)	(b)	(a)
(like כְּ-)	כְּמוֹשִׁיעֵנוּ like our Deliverer	כְּמַלְכֵּנוּ like our King	כַּאדוֹנֵינוּ like our Lord	כֵּאלֹהֵינוּ like our God
(to לְ-)	לְמוֹשִׁיעֵנוּ to our Deliverer	לְמַלְכֵּנוּ to our King	לַאדוֹנֵינוּ to our Lord	לֵאלֹהֵינוּ to our God
	מוֹשִׁיעֵנוּ our Deliverer	מַלְכֵּנוּ our King	אֲדוֹנֵינוּ our Lord	אֱלֹהֵינוּ our God

FIRST PART OF אֵין כֵּאלֹהֵינוּ (stanzas 1-3)

The first word

1. In the first stanza the first Hebrew word is: אֵין - (There is none)
2. In the second stanza the first Hebrew word is: מִי - (Who is?)
3. In the third stanza the first Hebrew word is: נוֹדֶה - (Let us give thanks)

(d)	(c)	(b)	(a)		
כְּמוֹשִׁיעֵנוּ...	כְּמַלְכֵּנוּ...	כַּאדוֹנֵינוּ...	כֵּאלֹהֵינוּ	אֵין	.1
... like our Deliverer	... like our King	...like our Lord	like our God	There is none	
כְּמוֹשִׁיעֵנוּ...	כְּמַלְכֵּנוּ...	כַּאדוֹנֵינוּ...	כֵּאלֹהֵינוּ	מִי	.2
... like our Deliverer	... like our King	...like our Lord	like our God	Who is	
לְמוֹשִׁיעֵנוּ...	לְמַלְכֵּנוּ...	לַאדוֹנֵינוּ...	לֵאלֹהֵינוּ	נוֹדֶה	.3
... to our Deliverer	...to our King	...to our Lord	to our God	Let us give thanks	

THE FIRST PART OF אֵין כֵּאלֹהֵינוּ

The message

1. אֵין - There is none   a) ... like our God   b)... like our Lord   c)... like our King   d)... like our Deliverer
2. מִי - Who is   a)... like our God?   b)... like our Lord?   c)... like our King?   d)... like our Deliverer?
3. נוֹדֶה - Let us give thanks   a)... to our God.   b)... to our Lord.   c)... to our King   d)... to our Deliverer

A PUZZLE

Now that we know the meaning of stanzas 1 - 3 let us stop and think for a moment:
Why does stanza 2 come after stanza 1?
Does it make sense? Can you figure out a reason for the sequence?

The answer is...

Look at the enlarged consonants in the box below; ignore the vowels. Read the large initial letters downward and you have created a new word. The word is ...

<table>
<tr><td>אָ</td><td>אָ</td><td>אָ</td><td>אָ</td></tr>
<tr><td>מֵ</td><td>מֵ</td><td>מֵ</td><td>מֵ</td></tr>
<tr><td>ן</td><td>ן</td><td>ן</td><td>ן</td></tr>
<tr><td>אֵין כְּמוֹשִׁיעֵנוּ</td><td>אֵין כְּמַלְכֵּנוּ</td><td>אֵין כַּאדוֹנֵינוּ</td><td>אֵין כֵּאלֹהֵינוּ</td></tr>
<tr><td>מִי כְמוֹשִׁיעֵנוּ</td><td>מִי כְמַלְכֵּנוּ</td><td>מִי כַאדוֹנֵינוּ</td><td>מִי כֵאלֹהֵינוּ</td></tr>
<tr><td>נוֹדֶה לְמוֹשִׁיעֵנוּ</td><td>נוֹדֶה לְמַלְכֵּנוּ</td><td>נוֹדֶה לַאדוֹנֵינוּ</td><td>נוֹדֶה לֵאלֹהֵינוּ</td></tr>
</table>

This is a popular device in Hebrew religious poetry known as acrostic.*
Stanzas 1, 2 and 3 had to be in this sequence, in order to spell אָמֵן

Why אָמֵן?

אֵין כֵּאלֹהֵינוּ is chanted at a point in the service when all prayers in the Shabbat morning service have been completed.**
At the end of each individual blessing we always say: אָמֵן
In order to mark the end of the entire service the author of אֵין כֵּאלֹהֵינוּ composed a grand אָמֵן in the form of an acrostic repeated four times.

---

* Some acrostics are based on the sequence of the alphabet and are known as alphabetical acrostics (see אַשְׁרֵי) Others may be based on the letters of the author's name and can be regarded as the "author's signature" (see לְכָה דוֹדִי and the "signature" of the author שְׁלֹמֹה הַלֵוִי).

** At the time when אֵין כֵּאלֹהֵינוּ was composed neither עָלֵינוּ nor אָדוֹן עוֹלָם was there yet to mark the end of the services.

4.   בָּרוּךְ = Blessed be   a) ... our God   b) ... our Lord   c) ... our King   d) ... our Deliverer.
5. אַתָּה הוּא = Thou art   a) ... our God   b) ... our Lord   c) ... our King   d) ... our Deliverer.

word acrostic

מוֹשִׁיעֵנוּ	בָּרוּךְ	מַלְכֵּנוּ	בָּרוּךְ	אֲדוֹנֵינוּ	בָּרוּךְ	אֱלֹהֵינוּ	בָּרוּךְ	4.
אַתָּה הוּא מוֹשִׁיעֵנוּ	מַלְכֵּנוּ הוּא אַתָּה	אֲדוֹנֵינוּ הוּא אַתָּה	אֱלֹהֵינוּ הוּא אַתָּה	5.

We are back at the beginning

A moment ago we sang the grand אָמֵן for the entire Jewish service; what are we doing now?
We are back at the beginning.
We proclaim: Our praise to God never really ends. As soon as a Jew says אָמֵן upon the completion of one prayer he is ready to start another prayer.

בָּרוּךְ אַתָּה ה' אֱלֹהֵינוּ מֶלֶךְ הָעוֹלָם...   ..... אָמֵן !

Jewish religious experience is circular. End and beginning meet.

אֵין כְּמוֹשִׁיעֵנוּ	אֵין כְּמַלְכֵּנוּ	אֵין כַּאדוֹנֵינוּ	אֵין כֵּאלֹהֵינוּ	.1
מִי כְּמוֹשִׁיעֵנוּ	מִי כְּמַלְכֵּנוּ	מִי כַאדוֹנֵינוּ	מִי כֵּאלֹהֵינוּ	.2
נוֹדֶה לְמוֹשִׁיעֵנוּ	נוֹדֶה לְמַלְכֵּנוּ	נוֹדֶה לַאדוֹנֵינוּ	נוֹדֶה לֵאלֹהֵינוּ	.3
בָּרוּךְ מוֹשִׁיעֵנוּ	בָּרוּךְ מַלְכֵּנוּ	בָּרוּךְ אֲדוֹנֵינוּ	בָּרוּךְ אֱלֹהֵינוּ	.4
אַתָּה הוּא מוֹשִׁיעֵנוּ	אַתָּה הוּא מַלְכֵּנוּ	אַתָּה הוּא אֲדוֹנֵינוּ	אַתָּה הוּא אֱלֹהֵינוּ	.5

Note: In the late Middle Ages the 5-stanza אֵין כֵּאלֹהֵינוּ was amplified by an additional stanza that deals with the incense-offering in the rites of the ancient Temple.

אַתָּה הוּא שֶׁהִקְטִירוּ אֲבוֹתֵינוּ לְפָנֶיךָ אֶת קְטֹרֶת הַסַּמִּים

13

WORDS WE SHOULD KNOW

Below is the standard beginning of all blessings. Most of these words of prayer are found in אֵין כֵּאלֹהֵינוּ

Blessed	בָּרוּךְ	בָּרוּךְ is found in stanza 4 of אֵין כֵּאלֹהֵינוּ
are You	אַתָּה	אַתָּה is in stanza 5
O Lord	אֲדֹנָי	Where is אֲדֹנָי ? אֲדֹנָי is the core part of
		אֲדוֹנֵינוּ — our Lord (stanza 5 and all stanzas)*
our God	אֱלֹהֵינוּ	אֱלֹהֵינוּ is in stanza 4 and in all the other stanzas too.
King of	מֶלֶךְ	מֶלֶךְ is also in every stanza. It is contained in the word מַלְכֵּנוּ
the Universe	הָעוֹלָם	הָעוֹלָם is the only word that does not appear in אֵין כֵּאלֹהֵינוּ

נוֹדֶה (= we give thanks) is related to the familiar word תּוֹדָה (thank you)

The Hebrew language does not use a separate word for "is."
("is" is implied)

מִי	=	who?	מִי	=	who is?
אֵין	=	none	אֵין	=	there is none
הוּא	=	he	הוּא	=	he is
אַתָּה	=	you	אַתָּה	=	you are
					(example: בָּרוּךְ אַתָּה ה'* = blessed are You O Lord)
בָּרוּךְ	=	blessed	בָּרוּךְ	=	blessed be
					(example בָּרוּךְ אֱלֹהֵינוּ blessed be our God)

---

* אֲדוֹנֵינוּ (= our Lord) is derived from אָדוֹן (= lord)
אֲדֹנָי is considered in Judaism the divine name. We translate it "Lord", with a capital "L".

Pronunciation: Out of deference to the divine name we pronounce it fully only in actual prayer or in reading from the Torah Scroll. On all other occasions we pronounce it "Hashem" (= the Name).

Spelling: In the prayerbook it is usually spelled יְיָ. See, however, a different spelling of the divine name in שְׁמַע and in various Psalms. ה' is the accepted spelling outside the prayerbook and the Bible. Our book will use the spelling ה'.

THE VOCABULARY OF THE PRAYERBOOK.

In order to comprehend the Hebrew of the prayerbook we need to discover a few of its rules.

Rule I: Hebrew is brief and condensed.
e.g. The two Hebrew words "אֵין כֵּאלֹהֵינוּ" are equivalent to six English words: "There is none like our God."

Rule II: The core of a Hebrew word is usually in the middle. The core is often surrounded by a "prefix" at the beginning and a "suffix" at the end.
In כֵּאלֹהֵינוּ (like our God) "כ" (=like) is a prefix and "נוּ" (=our) is a suffix.

When you see a Hebrew word that has a long English translation, look at the middle part of the word for a key to the central idea. (e.g. in כְּ מוֹשִׁיעַ נוּ, the key word מוֹשִׁיעַ is between the prefix (כ) and the suffix נוּ)

Rule III: In English, the adjective or pronoun comes before the noun (e.g. "our King"), whereas in Hebrew it comes after the noun. For example מַלְכֵּ נוּ "literally means "King our." (The suffix " נוּ " means "our.")

SEARCHING FOR THE BASIC WORD

	מוֹשִׁיעַ נוּ our Deliverer	מַלְכֵּ נוּ our King	אֲדוֹנֵי נוּ our Lord	אֱלֹהֵי נוּ our God
Core	מוֹשִׁיעַ Deliverer	מֶלֶךְ King	אָדוֹן Lord	אֱלֹהִים God
Suffix	נוּ our	נוּ our	נוּ our	נוּ our

Add the suffix נוּ by heart

בָּרוּךְ מוֹשִׁיעֵ...   בָּרוּךְ מַלְכֵּ...   בָּרוּךְ אֲדוֹנֵי...   בָּרוּךְ אֱלֹהֵי...

THE VOWELS CHANGE BUT THE MEANING REMAINS

כֵּאלֹהֵינוּ like our God (like כֵּ)	**כַּאדוֹנֵינוּ** like our Lord (like כַּ)	**כְּמַלְכֵּנוּ** like our King (like כְּ)	**כְּמוֹשִׁיעֵנוּ** like our Deliverer (like כְּ)	.1
כֵאלֹהֵינוּ like our God (like כֵ)	**כַאדוֹנֵינוּ** like our Lord (like כַ)	**כְמַלְכֵּנוּ** like our King (like כְ)	**כְמוֹשִׁיעֵנוּ** like our Deliverer (like כְ)	.2
לֵאלֹהֵינוּ to our God (to לֵ)	**לַאדוֹנֵינוּ** to our Lord (to לַ)	**לְמַלְכֵּנוּ** to our King (to לְ)	**לְמוֹשִׁיעֵנוּ** to our Deliverer (to לְ)	.3

<u>like = כ</u>

like = כְ   like = כְ   like = כַ   like = כַ   like = כֵ   like = כֵּ

<u>to = ל</u>

to = לְ   to = לֵ   to = לַ

Rule IV: In English, consonants and vowels are both important and indispensible to the meaning of a word, but not so in Hebrew. In Hebrew, consonants and vowels are not equal in importance. Consonants are decisive, but vowels are not. Vowels may change, yet the meaning remains unchanged.

1. כ = like but כ could be provided with different vowels (כֵ or כְ or כַ) and it would still mean "like". In addition the dot inside the כ may be removed, yet the meaning remains the same.

2. מַלְכֵּנוּ = our King "מַלְכֵּ " here means "King"; even though the basic word for "King" is מֶלֶךְ

<u>There is a method to those changes.</u>

Can the readers take the liberty of changing vowels and dots on their own? No.
There are reasons for these changes, but this requires advanced grammatical study. For our present purposes we know all the rules that we need to know.

16   See Vocabulary of Jewish life in Part II of the Book

עָלֵינוּ

Touro Synagogue at Newport.

עָלֵינוּ (in your סִדּוּר (p. 5)

Part I: THE ASSERTION *past + present tense*

The solemn introduction (lines 1-5)

1. a. It is (incumbent) upon us to extol the Lord of everything

   b. To pay homage to the shaper of the (world's) beginning

2. a. Who has not made us like the nations of other lands

   b. and has not fashioned us like (other) families of the earth;

3. a. Who has not fashioned our portion like theirs

   b. nor our destiny like all their multitudes.

4. a. For we bend our knee

   b. and bow and acknowledge

5. a. The supreme King of Kings

   b. The Holy One blessed be He.

1. a. עָלֵינוּ לְשַׁבֵּחַ לַאֲדוֹן הַכֹּל
  b. לָתֵת גְּדוּלָה לְיוֹצֵר בְּרֵאשִׁית
2. a. שֶׁלֹּא עָשָׂנוּ כְּגוֹיֵי הָאֲרָצוֹת
  b. וְלֹא שָׂמָנוּ כְּמִשְׁפְּחוֹת הָאֲדָמָה
3. a. שֶׁלֹּא שָׂם חֶלְקֵנוּ כָּהֶם
  b. וְגוֹרָלֵנוּ כְּכָל הֲמוֹנָם
4. a. וַאֲנַחְנוּ כּוֹרְעִים
  b. וּמִשְׁתַּחֲוִים וּמוֹדִים
5. a. לִפְנֵי מֶלֶךְ מַלְכֵי הַמְּלָכִים
  b. הַקָּדוֹשׁ בָּרוּךְ הוּא

Parallelism a/b same idea different words

The substance of the Assertion (lines 6-8)

6. a. He stretched forth the heavens
   b. and laid the foundations of the earth
7. a. The seat of His glory is visible in the heavens above,
   b. and the Presence of His might is manifest in the loftiest heights.
8. a. He is our God; there is none else.
   b. Truly He is our King, there is none besides Him.

   As it is written in His Torah:
9. a. Know this day,
   b. and consider it in your heart

The summary of the Assertion (line 10)

10. a. That the Lord is God in the heavens above
   b. and on the earth beneath, there is none other.

10. a. כִּי ה' הוּא הָאֱלֹהִים — בַּשָּׁמַיִם מִמַּעַל
   b. וְעַל הָאָרֶץ מִתָּחַת — אֵין עוֹד

כ like
ה the
ל to
נו us, our
לא no, not
ו and
ב on

PART II: THE HOPE *future*

T̶h̶e̶ complement the ASSERTION of Part I the second part expresses Hope: עַל כֵּן נְקַוֶּה (Therefore we hope)

Therefore we hope = עַל כֵּן נְקַוֶּה

11. We therefore hope in You, O lord our God,
    that we may soon behold the splendor of Your might
12a. when You will remove
    the abominations from the earth
12b. and when all idoltry
    will be utterly destroyed.
13a. (We hope for the day when) the world will be
    perfected under the reign of the Almighty,
    and all mankind will call upon Your name;
13b. when You will turn unto Yourself
    all the wicked of the earth.
14. May all the inhabitants of the world
    perceive and know

15a. that unto You every knee must bend
15b. every tongue vow allegiance.
16a. Before You, O Lord our God
    may they bend and prostrate themselves
16b. and to the glory of Your name,
    may they pay homage
17a. May they all accept the yoke of Your Kingship
    and may You reign over them speedily and
    forevermore.
17b. For the Kingdom is Yours
    and to all eternity You will reign in glory;
18a. as it is written in Your Torah;
    The Lord shall reign forever and ever.

THE SUMMARY
OF THE HOPE

18b. And it has been foretold;
The Lord shall become King over
all the earth;
on that day the Lord shall be
One and His name One

18b וְנֶאֱמַר
וְהָיָה ה׳ לְמֶלֶךְ עַל־כָּל־הָאָרֶץ
בַּיּוֹם הַהוּא יִהְיֶה ה׳ אֶחָד וּשְׁמוֹ אֶחָד

on
day

19

עָלֵינוּ consists of two parts.

Part I (beginning with the words עָלֵינוּ לְשַׁבֵּחַ) makes an assertion.

Part II (beginning with the words עַל כֵּן נְקַוֶה) expresses hope.

Prayer is often voiced in poetic form.

אֵין כֵּאלֹהֵינוּ uses the poetic device of acrostics. עָלֵינוּ uses the device of parallelism, which occurs very often in the Bible (and is therefore known as "biblical parallelism"); it creates a rhythm of great solemnity.

Each stanza of עָלֵינוּ consists of 2 "parallel" phrases (a,b). Phrase "b" expands and intensifies the imagery and the impact of phrase "a".

The sound of נוּ

In אֵין כֵּאלֹהֵינוּ we spoke of אֱלֹהֵינוּ, אֲדוֹנֵינוּ, מַלְכֵּנוּ, מוֹשִׁיעֵנוּ

In עָלֵינוּ we encounter עָלֵינוּ (1a), עָשָׂנוּ (2a), שָׂמָנוּ (2b), חֶלְקֵנוּ (3a), גוֹרָלֵנוּ (3b)

The suffix נוּ occurs in the prayerbook with great frequency. The sound of נוּ permeates the atmosphere of the prayerbook and the synagogue. It is more than a point of grammar. It is a Jewish ethnic and ethical message; it is one of the great assertions of our mutual interdependence. The life, the faith, the prayers and the hopes of the individual Jew are interwined with those of the community.

A Jew speaks more frequenty of "our" God (אֱלֹהֵינוּ) than of "my" God. Jewish prayer takes place mostly between the Jewish community and God.

Comparison and Analysis	New Words		Words with a familiar ring	Words we know		line
עָלֵינוּ = עַל נוּ ys on	(It is incumbent) upon us	עָלֵינוּ		Lord of	אֲדוֹן	1a
	all; everything	הַכֹּל				1a
	no	לֹא				2a
	no	לֹא				2b
	no	לֹא				3a
כְּכָל = כְּ כָל	like all	כְּכָל				3b
מִמֶּלֶךְ מַלְכֵי הַמְּלָכִים (in hymn שָׁלוֹם עֲלֵיכֶם)			מֶלֶךְ מַלְכֵי הַמְּלָכִים Supreme King of Kings	King	מֶלֶךְ	5a
				blessed be	בָּרוּךְ	5b
	the holy one	הַקָּדוֹשׁ				
				he	הוּא	5b
				the Lord	ה'	10a
				he is	הוּא	10a
				the God	הָאֱלֹהִים	10a
בַּשָּׁמַיִם = בַּ שָׁמַיִם	in heavens	בַּשָּׁמַיִם				10a
הָאָרֶץ = הָ אָרֶץ	the earth	הָאָרֶץ				10b
	on	עַל				10b
				there is none	אֵין	10b
				the Lord	ה'	18b
				King	מֶלֶךְ	
				the earth	הָאָרֶץ	
בְּיוֹם = בַּ יוֹם	on the day	בְּיוֹם		on	עַל	
	one	אֶחָד		all	כָּל	

The assertion of אֵין כֵּאלֹהֵינוּ "there is none like our God" finds a more elaborate expression in the ancient prayer of עָלֵינוּ : He is our God; He is our King; there is no other — anywhere — either in heaven or on earth. We feel highly priveleged to be able to proclaim this truth.

עָלֵינוּ and אֵין כֵּאלֹהֵינוּ compared.

While the assertion of God's unity in אֵין כֵּאלֹהֵינוּ is very succinct and almost playful, the assertion in עָלֵינוּ bears an air of profound thoughtfulness, solemnity, defiance and national pride. It is also coupled with the expression of a Messianic hope. Altogether it sounds like a Manifesto.
This Manifesto is epitomized by the summaries of Part I and Part II.

I. The Summary of Assertion

10. "The Lord is God in the Heavens above and on the Earth beneath. There is none other."

II. The Summary of Hope

18. "And the Lord shall be King over all the earth. On that day the Lord shall be One and His name One."

In history

a)   The prayer עָלֵינוּ was originally recited in the days of the Talmud as part of the מוּסָף service of רֹאשׁ הַשָּׁנָה. The initial composition of the prayer is said to go back even further into antiquity.

b)   In the Middle Ages during the Crusades it became the hymn of Jewish martyrs who refused to convert to Christianity. They went to their death defiantly, declaring: NOR We will not betray our religion, our belief in the One and Supreme God. We are happy to be ourselves, and would not exchange our lot for anyone else's lot, even at the price of our lives.

c)   Eventually עָלֵינוּ became the standard prayer at the conclusion of all daily prayers throughout the year. עָלֵינוּ undoubtedly expressed the prevailing mood of self-sacrificing zeal and joyful acceptance of Jewish commitments; it was therefore chosen as the fitting climax of all Jewish prayer services.

d)   Many of our ancestors gave their lives for this great assertion. Generations of their descendants were reared on the great hope: On that day the Lord shall be One and His name One.

Synagogue procedure

At the words וַאֲנַחְנוּ כּוֹרְעִים ("and we bend the knee") we bow towards the Ark.

AN OVERVIEW OF THE SHABBAT MORNING SERVICE:

The Shabbat Morning Service consists of three major sections:

Section 1 — שַׁחֲרִית *morning*   Section 2 — Torah Service   Section 3 — מוּסָף

Section 1: שַׁחֲרִית — during the early part of the morning.

Introductory Prayers	A. "Dawn" Blessings for early morning —	pp... 2	בִּרְכוֹת הַשַּׁחַר (="בְּרכוֹת")
	B. Chapters (and verses) of Song —	pp...54	פְּסוּקֵי דְזִמְרָא
The main Prayers	C. Sh'ma and its accompanying blessings	pp... 346	שְׁמַע
	D. עֲמִידָה (= the standing prayer) also called	pp... 354	עֲמִידָה

שְׁמוֹנֶה עֶשְׂרֵה and Silent Devotion

Section 2: Torah Service

The main parts of the Torah Service:

A. Taking out the Torah   הוֹצָאַת הַתּוֹרָה (pp. 394)
B. Reading from it the relevant portion   קְרִיאַת הַתּוֹרָה pp. 400- and בִּרְכוֹת הַתּוֹרָה
                                                                402
C. Returning it to the Ark.   הַכְנָסַת הַתּוֹרָה (pp. 414)

Section 3: מוּסָף

The מוּסָף section is the least complicated of the three sections

A. עֲמִידָה   (pp. 430)
B. concluding hymns   (pp. 508)

See "Vocabulary of Jewish life" in Part II

אֲדוֹן עוֹלָם

Each line of אֲדוֹן עוֹלָם ends with a rhyming syllable. Musically, it enjoys an enormous versatility.

This poem has certain rhythmic peculiarities. Most of the words (with minor exceptions) are 2-syllable words. Almost any melody can be made to fit the text.

שִׂים שָׁלוֹם

שָׁלוֹם is one of the ultimate yearnings of the Jew.

Part I God in the Universe

1.	He is the Lord of the Universe who reigned Before any being was created.	.אֲדוֹן עוֹלָם אֲשֶׁר מָלַךְ בְּטֶרֶם כָּל יְצִיר נִבְרָא
2.	At the time when all was made by his will, He was acknowledged as the King.	.לְעֵת נַעֲשָׂה בְחֶפְצוֹ כֹּל אֲזַי מֶלֶךְ שְׁמוֹ נִקְרָא
3.	And at the end, when all shall cease to be, God alone will awesomely reign.	.וְאַחֲרֵי כִּכְלוֹת הַכֹּל לְבַדּוֹ יִמְלוֹךְ נוֹרָא
4.	He was, He is, and He shall be In (eternal) splendor.	.וְהוּא הָיָה וְהוּא הֹוֶה וְהוּא יִהְיֶה בְּתִפְאָרָה
5.	He is One, and there is no other To compare to Him, or join with Him.	.וְהוּא אֶחָד וְאֵין שֵׁנִי לְהַמְשִׁיל לוֹ לְהַחְבִּירָה
6.	He is without beginning, without end; Might and mastery belong to Him.	בְּלִי רֵאשִׁית בְּלִי תַכְלִית וְלוֹ הָעֹז וְהַמִּשְׂרָה

Part II   God in my life

7.	He is my God, my living Redeemer the Rock of my destiny in times of distress.	.וְהוּא אֵלִי וְחַי גֹּאֲלִי וְצוּר חֶבְלִי בְּעֵת צָרָה
8.	He is my Banner and my Refuge My cup of bliss the day I call;	.וְהוּא נִסִּי וּמָנוֹס לִי מְנָת כּוֹסִי בְּיוֹם אֶקְרָא
9.	In His hand I entrust my soul When I sleep and when I wake.	.בְּיָדוֹ אַפְקִיד רוּחִי בְּעֵת אִישַׁן וְאָעִירָה
10.	As long as my soul is with my body, The Lord is with me; I shall not fear.	.וְעִם רוּחִי גְוִיָּתִי ה' לִי וְלֹא אִירָא

Notes.

אֲדוֹן עוֹלָם consists of two parts, which declare respectively,
1) He is, He was, and he will be
2) He is my Rock and my Protector

"He" (God) predominates in Part I (lines 1-6)
Part II (lines 7-10) abounds in "I" and "my". The Hebrew syllable י. recurs here ten times. Why? Because י. at the end of a Hebrew word means "my". Part II sings of "my God," "my soul," "my body," etc. There are not many such "personal" prayers in our prayerbook.

25

Comparison and Analysis		New Words	Words with a familiar ring		Words we know		line
Lord	אָדוֹן				Lord of	אֲדוֹן	1
everything	כֹּל הַכֹּל		everything	כָּל = הַכֹּל			
					universe	עוֹלָם	1
					King	מֶלֶךְ	2
	וְהוּא = וְ הוּא		and he	וְהוּא			4,4,5,7,8
					One	אֶחָד	5
	וְאֵין = וְ אֵין		and there is not	וְאֵין			
(My God,	אֵלִי, אֵלִי		my God	אֵלִי			7
my God =)			living	חַי			7
is the name of a			trouble; distress	צָרָה			7
classical Jewish					on the day	בְּיוֹם	8
folksong							

The ideas.

Philosophically

The ten lines of אֲדוֹן עוֹלָם present two themes.

    ① A cosmic theme: God in the Universe. (lines 1-6)

a.   God is beyond time. Before time, after time, and in time — God was, is, and will be — Past, Present, and Future.

b.   God is Creator and Master — Awesome, Magnificent, and Powerful.

    ② A personal theme: God in my life. (lines 7-10)

God is Trust, Rock, Refuge, Protection, Destiny, and Redemption.

Historically

אֲדוֹן עוֹלָם was composed in the 11th century. Its use grew in the course of time.

a.   It started out as a bedtime prayer (See lines 9-10) and traditional Jews use it until today at bedtime in conjunction with the reading of Sh'ma.

b.   The same lines, however, are appropriate for a prayer upon waking. In fact, since the 15th century אֲדוֹן עוֹלָם began to appear in prayerbooks at the very beginning of the morning service. (See in your prayerbook p.....)

c.   At the end of the 19th century, some congregations started using it at the very end of the service. It soon began to occupy a prominent place in the service. Its succinct affirmations and its philosophical and optimistic mood fitted beautifully with the new mood of that period. Some Jews felt more comfortable with the universailistic tone of אֲדוֹן עוֹלָם than with the exclusivist emphasis of עָלֵינוּ In time, it became the practice in all modern congregations to chant אֲדוֹן עוֹלָם after עָלֵינוּ on Shabbat and holidays.

Like עָלֵינוּ and unlike עָלֵינוּ

1   אֲדוֹן עוֹלָם emphasizes the assertion of God's unity:
The אֲדוֹן עוֹלָם proclaims: "He is One and there is no other to compare with Him or join with Him."

2   However, unlike עָלֵינוּ there is no nationalistic theme in אֲדוֹן עוֹלָם only a universal theme and a personal theme.

3   The contrast between the "plural" emphasis of עָלֵינוּ and the the emphasis on the "singular" in אֲדוֹן עוֹלָם is remarkable.

Central formulations

A number of the words and phrases of אֲדוֹן עוֹלָם contain central formulations of Jewish belief.

Reigned, reigns, will reign   1, 2, 3 מָלַךְ, מֶלֶךְ, יִמְלוֹךְ

Was, is, will be   *no "is" in Hebrew; play c tetragrammaton*   4 הָיָה, הֹוֶה, יִהְיֶה

He is my God and my living Redeemer.   7 הוּא אֵלִי וְחַי גֹּאֲלִי

27

שִׂים שָׁלוֹם (in your סִדּוּר on page 438~~ 362~~)

	English	Hebrew

1. Bestow peace, goodness, and blessing upon the world;   שִׂים שָׁלוֹם טוֹבָה וּבְרָכָה בָּעוֹלָם .1 *Siddur Sim Shalom*

2. grace, lovingkindness, and mercy   חֵן וָחֶסֶד וְרַחֲמִים .2

3. upon us and upon all Israel, Your people.   עָלֵינוּ וְעַל כָּל יִשְׂרָאֵל עַמֶּךָ .3

4. Bless us, O our Father, all of us together (- like one)   בָּרְכֵנוּ אָבִינוּ כֻּלָּנוּ כְּאֶחָד .4

5. with the light of Your Presence (Literally: countenance)   בְּאוֹר פָּנֶיךָ .5

6. For by the light of Your presence (literally: countenance) You gave us,   כִּי בְאוֹר פָּנֶיךָ נָתַתָּ לָּנוּ .6

7. O Lord, our God,   ה' אֱלֹהֵינוּ .7

8. a Torah of life, a love of kindness   תּוֹרַת חַיִּים וְאַהֲבַת חֶסֶד .8

9. and righteousness, blessing, mercy, life and peace.   וּצְדָקָה וּבְרָכָה וְרַחֲמִים וְחַיִּים וְשָׁלוֹם. .9

10. May it be good in Your sight (literally: "eyes") to bless Your people Israel.   וְטוֹב בְּעֵינֶיךָ לְבָרֵךְ אֶת עַמְּךָ יִשְׂרָאֵל .10

11. at all times and at all hours with Your peace.   בְּכָל עֵת וּבְכָל שָׁעָה בִּשְׁלוֹמֶךָ .11

12. Blessed be You , O Lord,   בָּרוּךְ אַתָּה ה' .12

13. Who blesses His people Israel with peace.   הַמְבָרֵךְ אֶת עַמּוֹ יִשְׂרָאֵל בַּשָּׁלוֹם. .13

שִׂים שָׁלוֹם was once the last prayer of the service.
It is now the last blessing of the עֲמִידָה.

28

Comparison and Analysis	New words	Words with a familiar ring	Words we know	line
			peace שָׁלוֹם	1,9
טוֹב		goodness טוֹבָה		1
and = וּ (וּ בְרָכָה)		and blessing וּבְרָכָה		1,9
in = בְּ (בָּ עוֹלָם)		in the world בָּעוֹלָם		1
charm חֵן	grace חֵן			2
and = וָ (וָ חֶסֶד)	and kindness וָחֶסֶד			2
and = וְ (וְ רַחֲמִים)	and mercy וְרַחֲמִים			2,9
			upon us עָלֵינוּ	3
			all כָּל	3
		Israel; יִשְׂרָאֵל the Jewish people		3
our Father, our King אָבִינוּ מַלְכֵּנוּ	our father אָבִינוּ			4
like = כְּ (כְּ אֶחָד)		like one כְּאֶחָד		4
			the Lord ה'	7,12
			our God אֱלֹהֵינוּ	7
תּוֹרָה		a Torah of... תּוֹרַת		8
to life לְחַיִים		life חַיִים		8,9
		righteousness; charity צְדָקָה		9
and = וְ (וְ טוֹב)		and it is good וְטוֹב		10
			blessed בָּרוּךְ	12
			are You אַתָּה	12
with = in = בַּ (בַּ שָׁלוֹם)		with peace בַּשָׁלוֹם		13

29

The ideas.

Many, many blessings, but above all — peace

In the early formative periods of the Jewish prayerbook, before עָלֵינוּ אֵין כֵּאלֹהֵינוּ and אֲדוֹן עוֹלָם were composed, the concluding prayer of the service was the last blessing of the עֲמִידָה the prayer שִׂים שָׁלוֹם Before that the final conclusion of the service in the ancient Temple in Jerusalem, used to be the priestly benediction.* שִׂים שָׁלוֹם is actually an elaboration and expansion of the priestly benediction. All the key thoughts of the priestly benediction (בִּרְכַּת כֹּהֲנִים) are present in שִׂים שָׁלוֹם

The Talmudic Sages say: the priestly benediction ends with שָׁלוֹם to indicate that none of the blessings are of any avail unless they are accompanied by Peace.**

Peace — individual, national and international

Our prayer שִׂים שָׁלוֹם follows immediately upon the priestly Benediction and reflects this Talmudic insight. It contains many blessings but שָׁלוֹם recurs again and again as a refrain (lines 1,9,11,12). It is interesting to note that the priestly benediction was couched in the singular and was directed at the individual Jew, but the prayer שִׂים שָׁלוֹם was spoken on behalf of the "entire people Israel" (lines 3,10,13). Modern prayerbooks have gone a step further and have added בָּעוֹלָם (= in the world) at the end of line 1. We pray of course for peace within our Jewish ranks but we pray for peace in the world as well.

Yearning

Peace has been one of Judaism's great yearnings. At all times and in all places we were victims of war. The prophet Isaiah has instilled in us the dream of peace.***

---

*The priestly benediction:
1. May the Lord bless you and keep you (יְבָרֶכְךָ ה' וְיִשְׁמְרֶךָ)
2. May the Lord make His countenance shine upon you and be gracious unto you.
3. May the Lord lift His countenance upon you and grant you peace."
**Source: Midrash — *Sifrei, Naso*
***Isaiah 2:4 —
"And they shall beat their swords into plowshares
and their spears into pruning hooks.
Nation shall not lift sword against nation
Neither shall they learn war any more."

See Vocabulary of Jewish Life, in Part II of the book

THE TORAH SERVICE

The Torah reading is the center of the Saturday morning service. A portion of the תוֹרָה is read in the synagogue each Shabbat morning.

 The actual reading of the Torah is preceded and followed by a medley of various prayer sentences and beatuiful tunes which evoke a great deal of audience participation.
Not all of these passages deal with the Torah theme.

Our unit will deal with three of these passages which deal specifically with the Torah.

A. One is sung in front of the open Ark before the Torah is taken out.
B. Another is sung when the Torah is lifted and displayed to the people upon the completion of the reading.
C. The third is sung before the open Ark, upon returning the Torah.

A. UPON TAKING OUT THE TORAH הוֹצָאַת הַתּוֹרָה

The key passage וַיְהִי בִּנְסֹעַ which is sung before the open Ark consists of three sentences. While they all deal with תּוֹרָה they relate to three different periods of history.

1. **וַיְהִי בִּנְסֹעַ** - (p. 394 in your prayerbook)

As the Ark travelled, Moses would say:
Arise, O Lord, and may Your enemies be scattered
And may Your adversaries flee before You

וַיְהִי בִּנְסֹעַ הָאָרוֹן וַיֹּאמֶר מֹשֶׁה
קוּמָה ה׳ וְיָפֻצוּ אוֹיְבֶיךָ
וְיָנֻסוּ מְשַׂנְאֶיךָ מִפָּנֶיךָ *

2. For out of Zion shall come forth Torah
and the word of God out of Jerusalem

כִּי מִצִּיּוֹן תֵּצֵא תוֹרָה
וּדְבַר ה׳ מִירוּשָׁלָיִם **

3. Praised be He, who in His holiness gave the Torah
to His people Israel

בָּרוּךְ שֶׁנָּתַן תּוֹרָה
לְעַמּוֹ יִשְׂרָאֵל בִּקְדוּשָׁתוֹ

---

*   Source: Numbers 10:35
** Source: Isaiah 2:3

B. UPON LIFTING THE TORAH   הַגְבָּהָה

As the Torah scroll is lifted and three columns of writing are displayed before the congregation the worshippers proclaim in song: (see p. 4ו0 in your prayerbook)

And this is the Torah which Moses set	וְזֹאת הַתּוֹרָה אֲשֶׁר שָׂם מֹשֶׁה
before the children of Israel	לִפְנֵי בְּנֵי יִשְׂרָאֵל
by the command (literally: "by the mouth") of God, through the hand of Moses	עַל פִּי ה׳ — בְּיַד מֹשֶׁה

C. UPON RETURNING THE TORAH — הַכְנָסַת הַתּוֹרָה

The תּוֹרָה is considered the source of our spiritual life, the symbolic tree of the eternal life and miraculous staying power.
As we return the תּוֹרָה to the Ark we sing (see p. 426 in your prayerbook)

The Torah is a tree of life to those who uphold it	עֵץ חַיִּים לַמַּחֲזִיקִים בָּהּ
and those who support it are happy.	וְתוֹמְכֶיהָ מְאוּשָׁר.
Its ways are ways of pleasantness	דְּרָכֶיהָ דַרְכֵי נוֹעַם
and all its paths are peace.	וְכָל נְתִיבוֹתֶיהָ שָׁלוֹם.
Turn us unto You, O Lord, and we shall return	הֲשִׁיבֵנוּ ה׳ אֵלֶיךָ וְנָשׁוּבָה.
Renew our days as of old.	חַדֵּשׁ יָמֵינוּ כְּקֶדֶם.

Comparison and Analysis	New Words	Words with a familiar ring	Words we know
אֲרוֹן קֹדֶשׁ = The Holy Ark from ⟨ = מִ ⟩ מִצִּיוֹן = מִ צִיּוֹן	The Ark הָאָרוֹן	Moses מֹשֶׁה From Zion מִצִּיוֹן From Jerusalem מִירוּשָׁלַיִם	Torah תּוֹרָה the Lord ה׳ blessed בָּרוּךְ Israel יִשְׂרָאֵל
בְּנֵי בְּרִית = Children of the Covenant בְּ יַד = בְּיַד *in*		בְּנֵי יִשְׂרָאֵל the children of Israel; the Jewish people in the hand = בְּיַד by the hand	
	Tree עֵץ		
עֵץ חַיִּים = Tree of life			life = חַיִּים peace = שָׁלוֹם

TORAH . ORNAMENTS. *Crown, mantle, finials, Italy, 17 and 18th century.*

34

ו, וְ and
בְּ in; with; on
כְּ like
לְ to
הַ the
לֹא = no
נוּ us; our

The Torah service contains elements of dialogue, education and pageantry.

In שַׁחֲרִית and מוּסָף we pray to God; in the Torah reading we listen to God.

The Torah service provides an opportunity for the total community to engage in an ongoing process of learning the basic sources of Judaism.

The pageantry is both auditory and visual: Opening the Ark, carrying the סֵפֶר תּוֹרָה , kissing it, singing about it, "going up to it," chanting the blessings; then reading the Scroll, lifting it, marching with it and finally returning it back to the Holy Ark (אֲרוֹן הַקֹּדֶשׁ).

All this creates an emotional uplift and contributes to the pride and joy of feeling Jewish.

A . Upon taking out the Torah

When the Ark is opened the floodgates of emotion and memory overwhelm us. Across space and time we recall three different moments in our history — and not necessarily in the proper sequence.

1.   Marching through the wilderness — on the way to the Promised Land — with the Holy Ark as guide.
2.   Proclaiming Torah to the world from the heights of Zion — through the mouths of the prophets.
3.   The supreme moment when God gave us the Torah at Sinai.

A1. Travelling with the Torah

Unlike the stationary Ark of today, the Ark in the days of Moses was portable. In the days of Moses the Holy Ark always travelled ahead of the people as the Jews proceeded from one station in the wilderness to the next.

As the Ark travelled, Moses would say:

"Arise O Lord and may your enemies be scattered and Your adversaries flee before you."*

The travelling Ark gave the Israelites a feeling of great courage. In the face of this uncommon courage their powerful enemies were overwhelmed by fear.

Generations later, whenever the Torah was carried through the congregation Jews relived the march in the wilderness under Moses and they kissed the סֵפֶר תּוֹרָה with reverence and love. With the Torah in their midst, they felt triumphant: Here marches our secret weapon that assured our survival through the millennia of dangerous encounters. With Torah, we shall continue to travel fearlessly into the millennia of the future.

*Source: Numbers 10:35 (קוּמָה ה' וְיָפֻצוּ אוֹיְבֶיךָ וְיָנֻסוּ מְשַׂנְאֶיךָ מִפָּנֶיךָ)

A2. A fact, a vision, and a hope

Whenever we see the Torah, we think of its powerful influence throughout the centuries. We recall the ancient prophets who exhorted the people in Zion to be true to the vision of Torah. Their doing so transformed Zion into the center of the Jewish spirit. Ever since the Prophet Isaiah the Jews began to view Zion (= Jerusalem) as the permanent source of their spiritual life and as the inexhaustible fountainhead of Torah. The hope and dream of Zion and of Torah have become inextricably intertwined. "For out of Zion shall come forth Torah and the word of God out of Jerusalem"*

A3. May God be blessed

Whenever we see the Torah our thoughts go back to that great moment at Sinai; it was the greatest and proudest moment in our collective life as a people. "Praised be He who in His holiness gave the Torah to His people Israel."

בָּרוּךְ שֶׁנָּתַן תּוֹרָה לְעַמּוֹ יִשְׂרָאֵל

B. Upon lifting the Torah (הַגְבָּהָה)

Theoretically every Jew is expected to read the Torah portion directly from the handwritten Scroll of the סֵפֶר תּוֹרָה. Yet, we only "call up" 7 Aliyot plus Maftir on any שַׁבָּת. The rest of the people follow the reading from a printed copy of the Pentateuch. In order to fulfill, if only symbolically, the requirement of reading directly from the Scroll, the Torah is lifted high and three columns of its writing are exhibited to the public view. After this symbolic "reading" the congregation joyously exclaims: "This is the Torah bestowed by Moses upon the children of Israel, by the command of God! through the hands of Moses."

C. Upon returning the תּוֹרָה to the Ark (הַכְנָסַת הַתּוֹרָה)

As the Torah pageant is completed we experience a warm sense of happiness. There is a feeling of sweetness and peacefulness about the Torah ("Her ways are ways of pleasantness and all her paths are peace").

דְּרָכֶיהָ דַרְכֵי נוֹעַם וְכָל נְתִיבוֹתֶיהָ שָׁלוֹם

We have been in the presence of the mysterious force that is the source of our vitality, eternality, and happiness.

Happiness is...
"The Torah is a Tree of Life to those who uphold it
and those who support her are happy"
We end on a note of nostalgia:
"Turn us unto You O Lord and we shall return. Renew our days as of old"

*Source: Isaiah 2:3 (כִּי מִצִּיּוֹן תֵּצֵא תוֹרָה וּדְבַר ה' מִירוּשָׁלָיִם)

THE WEEKLY TORAH READING. HOW IT GREW.

The original Biblical plan

The Five Books of Moses envisioned a democratic ideal of universal education. According to this revolutionary ideal, every parent was supposed to be the teacher of his own children* and once in seven years the entire people would assemble for a public reading of the Torah.**   However, we have no evidence that this initial plan actually worked. The prophets, the highly inspired interpreters of the ethical message of the Torah, arose in Israel from time to time to bring about a revival of the spirit.

The Ezra Plan

Upon the establishment of the Second Commonwealth, after the return from Babylonian exile, a new plan was needed to make the Torah the common possession of every Jew. Ezra the Scribe, one of the main leaders of that day, initiated such a new plan: to read portions of the Five Books of Moses, publicly and frequently on an ongoing basis.

The Ezra Plan has undergone various developments since its inception.

The Weekly Torah Reading

The סֵפֶר תּוֹרָה (Book of the Torah) is skillfully handwritten (or rather hand printed) on a parchment scroll by a Scribe (סוֹפֵר) It is kept in the Holy Ark אֲרוֹן הַקֹּדֶשׁ

The Five Books of Moses are divided into weekly portions corresponding approximately to the number of weeks of the year.

The weekly portions are read, or rather chanted, in sequence every Shabbat   by a skilled Torah Reader (בַּעַל קְרִיאָה) in accordance with the special musical notations called "Troppe."

While the בַּעַל קְרִיאָה reads the weekly portion from the סֵפֶר תּוֹרָה the congregants follow the reading from the printed text of the חוּמָשׁ (Pentateuch), that contains the Five Books of Moses (plus the text of the הַפְטָרוֹת).

* Source: Sh'ma (Deuteronomy 6:7 — "And you shall teach them diligently to your children").
** Source: Deuteronomy 31:10-13

An Aliyah to the Torah is a supreme honor.

According to the early Jewish philosopher, Saadia Gaon, the Jews are a nation by virtue of their Torah. Indeed according to the Bible the physical liberation of the Jews from Egyptian slavery had as its end goal the spiritual confrontation at Mt. Sinai (Exodus 3:12).

Aliyot

The weekly portion (סְדְרָה) is subdivided into seven small sections.

For each such section, one person in the congregation is honored to "go up" to the elevated Synagogue platform (בִּימָה) from which the Torah is read.

The honoree chants the blessings over the Torah.

The act of "going up" is called by the Hebrew name עֲלִיָה However, the section read is also referred to as an עֲלִיָה (We speak about "getting" or "being called up for" the third עֲלִיָה, the fourth עֲלִיָה etc.)

Traditionally Aliyot 1 and 2 are reserved for a Kohen and a Levite; they are not called up for Aliyot 3-7.
1) A Kohen (כֹּהֵן) gets the first עֲלִיָה 2) A Levite (לֵוִי) gets the second עֲלִיָה. An "Israelite" יִשְׂרָאֵל gets any of the עֲלִיוֹת 3-7, but not 1 and 2. Most of us are Israelites. (Note: Every Jew is an Israelite, including the כֹּהֵן and לֵוִי . However, for purposes of an Aliyah, the designation יִשְׂרָאֵל has been used for a Jew who is *not* a כֹּהֵן or לֵוִי)

Aliyot 3-7 are referred to by their numerical designation in Hebrew.

The 3rd Aliyah	שְׁלִישִׁי
4th Aliyah	רְבִיעִי
5th Aliyah	חֲמִישִׁי
6th Aliyah	שִׁשִּׁי
7th Aliyah	שְׁבִיעִי

After the seventh Aliyah, there ia s short עֲלִיָה called מַפְטִיר (the Concluder). It is usually a rereading of the last 3-4 sentences of the seventh עֲלִיָה

The person who is called up for מַפְטִיר also chants the הַפְטָרָה (a concluding chapter from the Prophets).

At the conclusion of the Torah reading, there is a הַגְבָּהָה (lifting) and a גְּלִילָה (rolling) of the Torah Scroll.

UNIT 5.

THE TORAH BLESSINGS
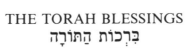

בָּרְכוּ אֶת ה'
הַמְבֹרָךְ
בָּרוּךְ ה'
הַמְבֹרָךְ
לְעוֹלָם וָעֶד

TORAH BLESSINGS FOR THE ALIYAH (p   in your prayerbook)

AA. Introductory Phrases (Call to Congregation and Response)

1. Bless the Lord who is blessed!	בָּרְכוּ אֶת ה׳ — הַמְבוֹרָךְ	I. (Honoree)
IIa. Blessed be the Lord - who is blessed forever and ever	בָּרוּךְ ה׳ — הַמְבוֹרָךְ לְעוֹלָם וָעֶד	IIa. (Congregational response)
IIb. Blessed be the Lord - who is blessed forever and ever	ברוך ה׳ — המבורך לעולם ועד	IIb. (Honoree repeats)

A. (Before reading of the Torah portion.)

1. Blessed are You, O Lord our God, King of the Universe	בָּרוּךְ אַתָּה ה׳ — אֱלֹהֵינוּ מֶלֶךְ הָעוֹלָם	1.
2. Who has chosen us — from all the peoples	אֲשֶׁר בָּחַר בָּנוּ — מִכָּל הָעַמִּים	2.
3. and has given us — His Torah.	וְנָתַן לָנוּ — אֶת תּוֹרָתוֹ	3.
4. Blessed are You, O Lord — Giver of the Torah	בָּרוּךְ אַתָּה ה׳ — נוֹתֵן הַתּוֹרָה	4.

B. (After the reading of the Torah portion.)

1. Blessed are You, O Lord our God, King of the Universe	ברוך אתה ה׳ אלהינו מלך העולם	1.
2. Who has given us — a Torah of truth	אֲשֶׁר נָתַן לָנוּ תּוֹרַת אֱמֶת	2.
3. and life eternal — has He planted within us.	וְחַיֵּי עוֹלָם נָטַע בְּתוֹכֵנוּ	3.
4. Blessed are You O Lord — Giver of the Torah	ברוך אתה ה׳ נותן התורה	4.

Notes.

Many of the newer prayerbooks prefer to translate בָּרוּךְ praised be
When the material is familiar the reader can read the text accurately without actually seeing the vowel signs. (The text inside the Torah Scroll carries no vowels; the Torah Reader — בַּעַל קְרִיאָה — is familiar with the text and he does not need to see the vowel).

Comparison and Analysis	New Words	Words with a familiar ring	Words we already know	line
			Blessed are You O Lord our God King of the Universe בָּרוּךְ אַתָּה ה׳ אֱלֹהֵינוּ מֶלֶךְ הָעוֹלָם	
eternity = עוֹלָם unto eternity; forever = לְעוֹלָם לְעוֹלָם וָעֶד forever and ever	לְעוֹלָם וָעֶד unto all eternity; forever and ever			AA
	חוֹר chose בָּחַר			A2
people = עַם (עַם יִשְׂרָאֵל חַי)	the nations הָעַמִּים			A2
		his Torah תּוֹרָתוֹ		A3
	he gives נוֹתֵן			A4
תּוֹרָה		Torah of.. תּוֹרַת		B2
		truth אֱמֶת		B2
	eternity עוֹלָם			B3

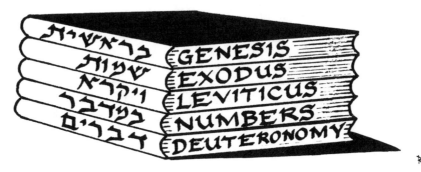

The Torah blessings incorporate a number of basic convictions of the Jewish tradition. As we come up to the Torah we become aware that our Torah is the starting point of our life as a people.

We feel deeply privileged that God has chosen us	בָּחַר בָּנוּ
from all other nations	מִכָּל הָעַמִּים
and gave us His Torah	וְנָתַן לָנוּ אֶת תּוֹרָתוֹ
which is a Torah of truth	תּוֹרַת אֱמֶת
and by doing so he planted in our midst a life of eternity	חַיֵּי עוֹלָם
While we are grateful to our God for many things we are particularly grateful	
that He is the Giver of the Torah	נוֹתֵן הַתּוֹרָה

The chosen people or choosing people?

The Bible says: "chosen". The Talmud says: "choosing."

According to the Biblical account (Exodus 19:4,6): ——Prior to the Giving of the Ten Commandments, God said: "I bore you on eagles' wings and brought you unto Me. Now... if you keep My covenant then you shall be Mine own treasure from among all the peoples... and you shall be unto Me a Kingdom of priests and a holy nation."

Conclusion: God has chosen Israel: yet God has chosen Israel, not for any political domination, but for a spiritual destiny; the Torah has been the guide of this chosen destiny. This is clearly implied in Exodus 19 and in numerous other Biblical statements.

According to a Talmudic view* God had offered the Torah to many nations, but they all refused to accept it. When He brought the Torah to the Jews they eagerly responded: "We shall do and we shall obey" (Exodus 24:7).

Conclusion: Israel has chosen God and His Torah.

The consensus of tradition: both chosen and choosing.

Jewish tradition has adopted the view that the Jewish people were both a chosen people and a choosing people. In every generation when a Jew reads Torah and studies Torah, when he loves Torah and lives the way of Torah, he is again choosing and being chosen.

---

*Source: Midrash — Sifrei, "V'zot Hab'rachah"

FOR YOUR ENRICHMENT

The Idiom of our People

Every culture contains certain unique idiomatic expressions that roll off the tongue of the speaker, automatically. The Hebrew expressions listed below are representative of the idiom of the prayerbook. They have become part of our cultural heritage.

אֲשֶׁר בָּחַר בָּנוּ	בָּרְכוּ אֶת ה׳ הַמְבוֹרָךְ
מִכָּל הָעַמִּים	לְעוֹלָם וָעֶד
תּוֹרַת אֱמֶת	בָּרוּךְ אַתָּה ה׳
נוֹתֵן הַתּוֹרָה	אֱלֹהֵינוּ מֶלֶךְ הָעוֹלָם

By heart

It is traditional to recite the Torah blessings by heart.
In the past when a student learned these blessings for the first time, the teacher would begin each phrase and the student would complete it.

AA. Introduction to first blessing

..... בָּרְכוּ אֶת ה׳

..... בָּרוּךְ ה׳ הַמְבוֹרָךְ לְעוֹלָם

..... בָּרוּךְ ה׳ הַמְבוֹרָךְ

B. Blessing after the reading of the Torah portion	A. Blessing before the reading of the Torah portion.
1. בָּרוּךְ אַתָּה ה׳ אֱלֹהֵינוּ	1. בָּרוּךְ אַתָּה ה׳ אֱלֹהֵינוּ מֶלֶךְ .....
2. אֲשֶׁר נָתַן לָנוּ תּוֹרַת	2. אֲשֶׁר בָּחַר ... מִכָּל .....
3. וְחַיֵּי עוֹלָם נָטַע	3. וְנָתַן לָנוּ אֶת .....
4. בָּרוּךְ אַתָּה ה׳ נוֹתֵן	4. בָּרוּךְ אַתָּה ה׳ נוֹתֵן .....

43

THE ALIYAH PROCEDURE

The procedure when you are called up to the סֵפֶר תּוֹרָה for an עֲלִיָה is as follows:

The Reader points to the appropriate spot in the Torah Schroll with a pointer (=יָד)

You:
1) Touch that spot with the צִיצִית of your טַלִית
2) Kiss the צִיצִית
3) Hold on to the wooden rollers(עֵץ חַיִּים) of the Scroll of the סֵפֶר תּוֹרָה
4) a. Chant the בָּרְכוּ introduction to the first blessing
   b. Wait for the congregational response
   c. Repeat the congregational response
   d. Finish the entire first blessing, solo.
   e. The Reader will read the עֲלִיָה on your behalf. You should follow along quietly.
5) At the conclusion of your עֲלִיָה you kiss the תּוֹרָה again, close the Scroll, and chant the 2nd blessing, while holding the עֵץ חַיִּים (wooden rollers)

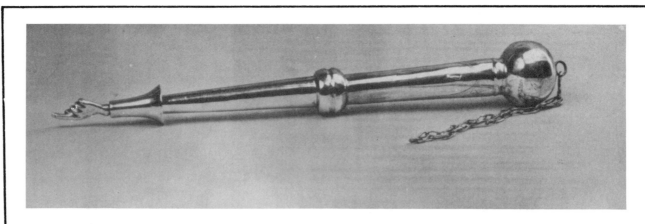

TORAH POINTER, Poland, 19th century

---

*The תּוֹרָה is called symbolically עֵץ חַיִּים (a tree of life.) As a result, the rollers of the Torah scrolls which are always made of wood (עֵץ) have been given the nickname "עֵץ חַיִּים"

שְׁמַע

שְׁמַע יִשְׂרָאֵל יְהוָה אֱלֹהֵינוּ יְהוָה אֶחָד
וְאָהַבְתָּ אֵת יְהוָה אֱלֹהֶיךָ בְּכָל לְבָבְךָ וּבְכָל נַפְשְׁךָ
וּבְכָל מְאֹדֶךָ וְהָיוּ הַדְּבָרִים הָאֵלֶּה אֲשֶׁר אָנֹכִי מְצַוְּךָ
הַיּוֹם עַל לְבָבֶךָ וְשִׁנַּנְתָּם לְבָנֶיךָ וְדִבַּרְתָּ בָּם בְּשִׁבְתְּךָ
בְּבֵיתֶךָ וּבְלֶכְתְּךָ בַדֶּרֶךְ וּבְשָׁכְבְּךָ וּבְקוּמֶךָ וּקְשַׁרְתָּם
לְאוֹת עַל יָדֶךָ וְהָיוּ לְטֹטָפֹת בֵּין עֵינֶיךָ וּכְתַבְתָּם עַל
מְזוּזוֹת בֵּיתֶךָ וּבִשְׁעָרֶיךָ

Since you already know the printed text of the first paragraph of שְׁמַע
you may try to read some of   this text in the facsimile.
This is the way the שְׁמַע looks in a תּוֹרָה or תְּפִלִין or מְזוּזָה.

45

שְׁמַע   (p..... in your prayerbook

1. Hear, O Israel: The Lord our God, the Lord is One!	שְׁמַע יִשְׂרָאֵל ה׳ אֱלֹהֵינוּ ה׳ אֶחָד	1.
2. (Blessed be the name of His glorious Kingship forever and ever)	(בָּרוּךְ שֵׁם כְּבוֹד מַלְכוּתוֹ לְעוֹלָם וָעֶד)	2.
3. And you shall love the Lord your God	וְאָהַבְתָּ אֵת ה׳ אֱלֹהֶיךָ	3.
4. With all your heart, with all your soul, and with all your might	בְּכָל לְבָבְךָ וּבְכָל נַפְשְׁךָ וּבְכָל מְאֹדֶךָ	4.
5. And these words which I command you this day	וְהָיוּ הַדְּבָרִים הָאֵלֶּה אֲשֶׁר אָנֹכִי מְצַוְּךָ הַיּוֹם	5.
6. shall be upon your heart.	עַל לְבָבֶךָ	6.
7. And you shall teach them diligently to your children.	וְשִׁנַּנְתָּם לְבָנֶיךָ	7.
8. And you shall speak of them —	וְדִבַּרְתָּ בָּם	8.
9. When you sit in your house	בְּשִׁבְתְּךָ בְּבֵיתֶךָ	9.
10. When you walk by the way	וּבְלֶכְתְּךָ בַדֶּרֶךְ	10.
11. When you lie down and when you rise up.	וּבְשָׁכְבְּךָ וּבְקוּמֶךָ	11.
12. And you shall bind them — for a sign upon your hand	וּקְשַׁרְתָּם לְאוֹת עַל יָדֶךָ	12.
13. And they shall be for frontlets between your eyes.	וְהָיוּ לְטֹטָפוֹת בֵּין עֵינֶיךָ	13.
14. And you shall write them —	וּכְתַבְתָּם	14.
15. Upon the doorposts of your house and upon your gates.	עַל מְזוּזוֹת בֵּיתֶךָ וּבִשְׁעָרֶיךָ	15.

Notes.

ONE   אֶחָד

The שְׁמַע consists of three passages. The first passage is the most important.
The quintessential proclamation of the Bible about the unity of God comes from the first sentence of the first passage:

שְׁמַע יִשְׂרָאֵל ה׳ אֱלֹהֵינוּ — ה׳ אֶחָד

MOSES IS SPEAKING TO YOU

שְׁמַע is more than a prayer; it is a solemn pronouncement.
In the first sentence (Hear, O Israel!), Moses is addressing the entire people of Israel.
However, the rest of the passage is directed to every single Israelite, to each individual, not just to the people as a whole. That is why sixteen words (above) end with the suffix ךָ (= yours). Five words contain the ending תָּ (you)

Note the parenthesis and the small print of line 2. This line is usually recited in a whisper.

Our growing vocabulary

Comparison and Analysis		New Words		Words with a familiar ring		Words we know		line
				Hear	שְׁמַע			1
						Israel	יִשְׂרָאֵל	1
						Lord	ה'	1,3
						our God	אֱלֹהֵינוּ	1
						one	אֶחָד	1
						Blessed be	בָּרוּךְ	2
		name	שֵׁם					2
glory	כָּבוֹד	glory of	כְּבוֹד					2
honor						forever	לְעוֹלָם וָעֶד	2
						and ever		3
		and you shall love	וְאָהַבְתָּ					3
				your God	אֱלֹהֶיךָ			3
בְּכָל = בְּ כָל				with all	בְּכָל			4
וּבְכָל = וּ בְּ כָל				and with all	וּבְכָל			4
הַיוֹם = הַ יוֹם				this day	הַיוֹם			6
						on; upon	עַל	6,12,15
hand	יָד			your hand	יָדְךָ			12
eye	עַיִן	Your eyes	עֵינֶיךָ					13
M'zuzah*	מְזוּזָה			doorposts	מְזוּזֹת			15

---

*Originally the word M'zuzah (מְזוּזָה) meant doorpost. In time the parchment scroll attached to the doorpost has acquired the name מְזוּזָה.
It is not the outside container, but the properly inscribed parchment scroll that constitutes the מְזוּזָה

The central theological belief of Judaism — proclaimed in the Sh'ma — is:

There is only one God in the World and our God is the One (אֶחָד)
The God of the Jews is the God of the Universe; the God of the Universe is the God of the Jews.

THE WITNESS = עֵד

In the Torah scroll the text of the great affirmation looks like the line below. Please note the enlarged letters in
שְׁמַע and אֶחָד

שמע ישראל יהוה אלהינו יהוה אחד

Tradition supplies a reason for that enlargement:
If you combine the enlarged letters you will see a new word: Witness = עֵד = ד plus ע*
Ever since the Revelation at Sinai every Jew considers himself a Witness to God's unity. Each time a Jew recites the Sh'ma he bears witness before the world that God is one and unique.
Each time a Jew recites the Sh'ma with "Kavanah" (= deep intent) the following classic story comes to mind:
The great scholar Rabbi Akiba was marching to a martyr's death for the "crime" of upholding Judaism. His face radiated with joy. His disciples asked him: Why are you so happy? Akiba replied, "All my life I have been yearning for the opportunity to love my God with all my heart, with all my soul, and all my might. This is the moment: I love my God mightily, even at the price of life itself."**

The Defiant Phrase (line 2)

The sentence בָּרוּךְ שֵׁם כְּבוֹד מַלְכוּתוֹ לְעוֹלָם וָעֶד ("Blessed be the glory of His Kingship forever and ever.") is printed in the prayerbook in small print. In our book it is printed in parenthesis. Why? Because it is not really part of the biblical text of שְׁמַע.
So why is it here at all? Therein lies a tale.

a) This phrase first appeared in the ritual of the ancient Temple as the people's response to the priests' call: Sh'ma = hear! Eventually this exclamation was absorbed into the original text.

b) The key word of the phrase is מַלְכוּתוֹ = His Kingship.
   In Jewish theology God is the King of the Universe and of the Jewish people. In the course of time, when certain Roman Emperors began to declare themselves as Gods and as Kings ruling over Judea, this Jewish declaration about God and His Kingship was no longer seen as a mere theological statement, but also as a defiant political statement against the Emperor of Rome.

In a whisper

However, for fear of the Romans overhearing it they began to recite this significant assertion in an inaudible whisper — except on Yom Kippur.
This whisper has remained a custom until today. It is a dual historic reminder both of our fears and our defiance during periods of persecution. At the same time, it reminds us that Rabbi Akiba would not whisper the שְׁמַע. He died a martyr with the שְׁמַע on his lips for all the world to hear.

48
*Source: Sefer Abudraham
**Source: Talmud — B'rachot 61b.

FOR YOUR ENRICHMENT

Some of the Key Words

1. Hear, O........ the Lord............. , the Lord is......!	1. שְׁמַע יִשְׂרָאֵל ה׳ אֱלֹהֵינוּ ה׳ אֶחָד
2. (Blessed be the name of His glorious.........forever and ever)	2. בָּרוּךְ שֵׁם כְּבוֹד מַלְכוּתוֹ לְעוֹלָם וָעֶד
3. And you shall love the Lord.............	3. וְאָהַבְתָּ אֵת ה׳ אֱלֹהֶיךָ
4. With all _your heart_ with all _your soul_ and with all your might	4. בְּכָל לְבָבְךָ וּבְכָל נַפְשְׁךָ וּבְכָל מְאֹדֶךָ
5. And these words which I command you......	5. וְהָיוּ הַדְּבָרִים הָאֵלֶּה אֲשֶׁר אָנֹכִי מְצַוְּךָ הַיּוֹם
6. shall be upon..........	6. עַל לְבָבֶךָ
7. And you shall teach them diligently............	7. וְשִׁנַּנְתָּם לְבָנֶיךָ
8. And you shall speak of them............	8. וְדִבַּרְתָּ בָּם
9. When you sit _in your house_	9. בְּשִׁבְתְּךָ בְּבֵיתֶךָ
10. When you walk by the way............	10. וּבְלֶכְתְּךָ בַדֶּרֶךְ
11. When you lie down and when you rise up..........	11. וּבְשָׁכְבְּךָ וּבְקוּמֶךָ
12. And you shall bind them for a _sign_ upon _the hand_	12. וּקְשַׁרְתָּם לְאוֹת עַל יָדֶךָ
13. And they shall be for frontlets between _your eyes_	13. וְהָיוּ לְטוֹטָפוֹת בֵּין עֵינֶיךָ
14. And you shall write them......	14. וּכְתַבְתָּם
15. Upon the........of ....and upon your gates............	15. עַל מְזוּזוֹת בֵּיתֶךָ וּבִשְׁעָרֶיךָ

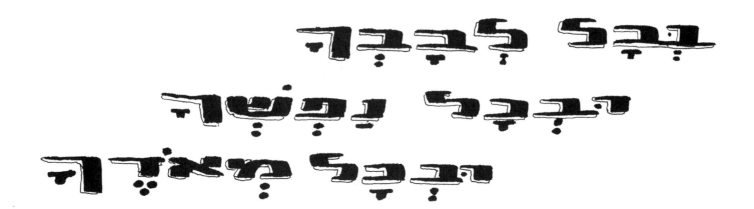

49

A SUMMARY OF THE COMMANDMENTS OF THE FIRST PARAGRAPH OF שְׁמַע

3-6 to love God and	וְאָהַבְתָּ אֵת ה׳ אֱלֹהֶיךָ
to take God's words to heart	וְהָיוּ הַדְּבָרִים הָאֵלֶּה עַל לְבָבֶךָ
7 to teach them to the children	וְשִׁנַּנְתָּם לְבָנֶיךָ
8-11 to speak of them at all times	וְדִבַּרְתָּ בָּם
12 to put on T'fillin on the hand	וּקְשַׁרְתָּם לְאוֹת עַל יָדֶךָ
13 to put on T'fillin on the head	וְהָיוּ לְטֹטָפוֹת בֵּין עֵינֶיךָ
14-15 to put "M'zuzot" on the doorposts	וּכְתַבְתָּם עַל מְזוּזוֹת בֵּיתֶךָ

Line 7 — The basis for intensive Jewish education

The two Hebrew words וְשִׁנַּנְתָּם לְבָנֶיךָ (and you shall teach them diligently to your children) have been responsible for the Jewish concept of universal education and for the resulting great Jewish passion for learning.

Line 8 — 11 — The Mitzvah of reading the Sh'ma daily (קְרִיאַת שְׁמַע)

In compliance with line 8-11, the reading of שְׁמַע became a primary component of our evening and morning prayers.

Line 12—13 — T'fillin — תְּפִלִּין

Inside the תְּפִלִּין are parchment scrolls which contain the first two paragraphs of שְׁמַע and two other paragraphs from the Bible which mention the תְּפִלִּין. These paragraphs are inscribed by the hand of a special Torah scribe (סוֹפֵר). T'fillin are traditionally worn by males over age 13 during weekday morning services, but not on Shabbat and holidays. תְּפִלִּין שֶׁל רֹאשׁ are worn on the head. תְּפִלִּין שֶׁל יַד are worn on the left arm. If a person is left-handed, the T'fillin are worn on the right arm.

Lines 14—15   M'zuzah.

The מְזוּזָה is placed in a diagonal position on the upper third of the doorpost on the right side of the entrance.
This slanted position makes it possible for the entering person to touch the M'zuzah conveniently. The מְזוּזָה is
a small parchment scroll upon which the first two passages of Sh'ma are inscribed by a Torah scribe (סוֹפֵר).
The outward container may be elaborate or simple, according to your taste.
But one must remember that the important thing is the scroll inside.

Tzitzit צִיצִית (see paragraph 3 of שְׁמַע)

The third paragraph of שְׁמַע (read in English pp 349 in your prayerbook) commands the putting on of fringes
(צִיצִית) on the four corners of our garments as reminders to obey God's מִצְווֹת (מִצְוֹת) Out of this command
grew the development of the prayer shawl (טַלִית) worn by males during the Morning Services.
Pious Jews also wear צִיצִית all day long, atached to a special garment called טַלִית קָטָן (a small Talit) or
אַרְבַּע כַּנְפוֹת (four corners).

51

HOW DO WE SAY THE שְׁמַע

Twice daily: שְׁמַע is recited in the morning prayers of שַׁחֲרִית (p.   in your prayerbook), and it is also recited in the evening service. (p.   in your prayerbook).

Before bedtime: Traditionally שְׁמַע is also recited before bedtime. ("When you are lying down"). שְׁמַע was the first prayer taught a Jewish child and every Jew knew שְׁמַע by heart from childhood. שְׁמַע addresses itself to each individual Jew, and each Jew took Sh'ma very personally and made it his own very special treasure.

On other occasions: The Jew also recited the Sh'ma on various occasions of crisis and of joy; at the cradle of a newborn baby; on the deathbed; when he found himself confronted with mortal danger; on occasions of martyrdom, etc.

Sitting or standing: Traditionally, שְׁמַע used to be recited at services, in a sitting position. However, in many modern congregations it is now recited standing.

Eyes closed: As the declaration of Jewish belief in God's unity it has been recited for generations with great intensity, with eyes closed for purposes of concentration. It was pronounced with strong emphasis on the letter ד of the אֶחָד (One) to make it unmistakably clear that God is One.

Whispering: The sentence בָּרוּךְ שֵׁם כְּבוֹד מַלְכוּתוֹ לְעוֹלָם וָעֶד is recited all year round in a whisper; except on Yom Kippur when it is recited aloud.

Touch the T'fillin: On weekdays some people would touch the T'fillin (תְּפִלִין) of the arm and the head when the reference to them was made in the שְׁמַע The תְּפִלִין are worn only on weekdays.

Touch the Tzitzit: In the daytime, when the טַלִית is worn, it is customary to hold the צִיצִית while reciting the Sh'ma. We kiss the צִיצִית each time that the צִיצִית are mentioned in the third paragraph of the שְׁמַע and when the final words of that paragraph are recited.

___

See Vocabulary of Jewish Life in Part II of this book

עֲמִידָה

The stairs leading to the entrance of the Machpelah Cave at Hebron,

THE FIRST OPENING BLESSING — (אָבוֹת FATHERS) (p   in your prayerbook)

1. Blessed are You O Lord	.1 בָּרוּךְ אַתָּה ה'
2. Our God and God of our Fathers	.2 אֱלֹהֵינוּ וֵאלֹהֵי אֲבוֹתֵינוּ
3. the God of Abraham	.3 אֱלֹהֵי אַבְרָהָם
the God of Isaac and	אֱלֹהֵי יִצְחָק
the God of Jacob	וֵאלֹהֵי יַעֲקֹב.
4. the God who is great, mighty and awesome,	.4 הָאֵל הַגָּדוֹל הַגִּבּוֹר וְהַנּוֹרָא
supreme God.	אֵל עֶלְיוֹן.
5. Who bestows good deeds of kindness	.5 גּוֹמֵל חֲסָדִים טוֹבִים
6. and although He is Master of Everything	.6 וְקוֹנֵה הַכֹּל
7. He still remembers the kind deeds of our Fathers.	.7 וְזוֹכֵר חַסְדֵי אָבוֹת
8. He will surely bring a redeemer to their children's children	.8 וּמֵבִיא גוֹאֵל לִבְנֵי בְנֵיהֶם
9. in love — for the sake of His Name.	.9 לְמַעַן שְׁמוֹ בְּאַהֲבָה.
10. O King who helps and delivers and shields.	.10 מֶלֶךְ עוֹזֵר וּמוֹשִׁיעַ וּמָגֵן.
11. Blessed are You, O Lord —	.11 בָּרוּךְ אַתָּה ה'
12. Shield of Abraham.	.12 מָגֵן אַבְרָהָם.
Notes.	

At the core of every Service (mornings, afternoons and evenings) is the עֲמִידָה — the "Standing Prayer" par excellence. In fact, on שַׁבָּת and holiday mornings we have two עֲמִידוֹת one for שַׁחֲרִית and one for מוּסָף. The עֲמִידָה is recited by the individual worshipper in a whispering voice. It therefore is often referred to as Silent Devotion.

Each עֲמִידָה begins with three Opening Blessings, ends with three Closing Blessings, and has a middle part comprising one or more blessings.
On שַׁבָּת the middle part consists of a single, long blessing.
Each of the Opening Blessings and Closing Blessings are identical in all עֲמִידוֹת.
The middle part varies in different עֲמִידוֹת for example, וְשָׁמְרוּ (see p....) belongs to the middle part of the עֲמִידָה of מוּסָף; יִשְׂמְחוּ (see p.....) belongs to the middle part of the עֲמִידָה of שַׁחֲרִית.

---

lines 3 and 7   "Fathers" = Patriarchs = ancestors.
line 8   children's children = descendants
line 9   His Name = His reputation.

SECOND OPENING BLESSING

1. You, O Lord, are mighty forever.

2. You bestow life upon the departed

3. You are great in deliverance.

5. (You cause the wind to blow and the rain to fall.)

5. You sustain the living — with kindness

6. and revive the dead — in great compassion

7. You support the falling,

8. You heal the sick,

9. You release the people who are in bondage,

10. And You keep faith with those who sleep in the dust.

11. Who is like unto You Master of mighty deeds?

12. Who can compare with You,

13. O King, who bestows death and life and brings deliverance?

14. Faithful are You to bestow life upon the departed.

15. Blessed are You, O Lord,

16. Who bestows life upon the dead.

1. אַתָּה גִּבּוֹר לְעוֹלָם ה'

2. מְחַיֵּה מֵתִים אַתָּה,

3. רַב לְהוֹשִׁיעַ.

4. (מַשִּׁיב הָרוּחַ וּמוֹרִיד הַגֶּשֶׁם).

5. מְכַלְכֵּל חַיִּים בְּחֶסֶד,

6. מְחַיֵּה מֵתִים בְּרַחֲמִים רַבִּים.

7. סוֹמֵךְ נוֹפְלִים

8. וְרוֹפֵא חוֹלִים

9. וּמַתִּיר אֲסוּרִים

10. וּמְקַיֵּם אֱמוּנָתוֹ לִישֵׁנֵי עָפָר.

11. מִי כָמוֹךָ בַּעַל גְּבוּרוֹת.

12. וּמִי דּוֹמֶה לָּךְ,

13. מֶלֶךְ מֵמִית וּמְחַיֵּה וּמַצְמִיחַ יְשׁוּעָה?

14. וְנֶאֱמָן אַתָּה לְהַחֲיוֹת מֵתִים.

15. בָּרוּךְ אַתָּה ה'

16. מְחַיֵּה הַמֵּתִים.

	Rosh Chodesh	Daily	Shabbat	Festivals	
		106	354	366	shacharit
		168	574	586	mincha
		210	296	304	ma'ariv
	486		430; 442 (alt.)	456	musaf

Notes.

God as redeemer
In Jewish theology God is on the side of the weak.
Throughout the prayerbook we reach out to God who:
    supports the falling סוֹמֵךְ נוֹפְלִים
    heals the sick רוֹפֵא חוֹלִים
    and releases the bound מַתִּיר אֲסוּרִים

Comparison and Analysis	New words	Words with a familiar ring	Words we already know	line
			blessed בָּרוּךְ	1,12 "אָבוֹת"
			are You אַתָּה	1,12
			o Lord ה'	1,12
God אֱלֹהִים			our God אֱלֹהֵינוּ	2
וֵ אלֹהֵי = וֵאלֹהֵי		and the God of וֵאלֹהֵי		2
אָבוֹת = אֲבוֹתֵי נוּ		our fathers אֲבוֹתֵינוּ		2
		Abraham אַבְרָהָם		3
		Isaac יִצְחָק		3
		Jacob יַעֲקֹב		3
House of God בֵּית אֵל		the God הָאֵל		4
My God! אֵלִי		God אֵל		4
	great גָּדוֹל	everything הַכֹּל		
אֲבוֹתֵינוּ ; אָבִינוּ		fathers אָבוֹת		7
			King מֶלֶךְ	10
Shield of David מָגֵן דָוִד (Star of David)	Shield מָגֵן			**10**
				"גְּבוּרוֹת"
			You; You are אַתָּה	1,2,14,15
			unto eternity לְעוֹלָם	1
			Lord ה'	1
	wind רוּחַ			4
	rain גֶּשֶׁם			4
			life חַיִּים	5
			kindness חֶסֶד	5
			mercy רַחֲמִים	6
			who מִי	11
וּמִי = וּ מִי		and who וּמִי		12
			King מֶלֶךְ	13
			blessed בָּרוּךְ	15

(handwritten note near line 10: heroism, greatness, indeed)

(handwritten note at bottom: 2 some vowel m... mu = generally accent is on the 1st)

The ideas.

THE FIRST OPENING BLESSING: "FATHERS" = אָבוֹת

Some of the blessings of the עֲמִידָה carry individual titles.

The title of the first Opening Blessing is אָבוֹת = Fathers.

God is our God and the God of our Fathers.

He remembers the merits of our ancestors and he will bring redemption to their grandchildren. He is Supreme, Master and Creator of Everything; the God of the world; and yet He is full of kindness, He remembers merit, and he rewards — with love.

He is helper, protector, and shield; the God of Abraham.

Traditionally, the Jew was always proud of the "merits of the Fathers" and he pleaded to God for special consideration on their account.

It is a deeply rooted concept and it reappears in many of our prayers.

It is also interesting that many Jewish prayers seem to emphasize contrast and supplementation. e.g., in Blessing No. 1 — Our God and God of our Fathers; God of the universe and God of the Jews.

Blessing No. 2 — (below): God of might and God of mercy; God of the living and God of the deceased.

Blessing No. 3 — (below): God is holy and the Jews are holy.**

THE SECOND OPENING BLESSING: "GOD'S MIGHT" = גְּבוּרוֹת

The Second Blessing speaks of God's great Might and Mercy and Kindness.

The subject is rain and life and death.

Israel always prayed with fervent anticipation for life-giving rain.***

The amount of rain made the difference between survival and starvation.

Rain was viewed as revival and rebirth in nature and as miraculous as resurrection.****

God's power is exercised through kindness and mercy.

God's kindness extends to both the living and the dead.

The Jew strongly believes in the immortality of the human soul.

The soul, which is a particle of the living, invisible, and everpresent God in us, returns to God.

The exact nature and form of the immortality have been subjects of debate and reinterpretation since time immemorial.

While some branches of Judaism hope for a future physical resurrection, other branches maintain that the creative soul retains a powerful immortal impact upon untold generations of the future.

---

*On weekdays, the middle part of the Amidah consists of 13 blessings. The weekday עֲמִידָה is usually called שְׁמוֹנֶה עֶשְׂרֵה (= 18) based on the original number of its benedictions, which used to be 18; now it is really 19 (3 + 13 + 3).

By force of habit even the עֲמִידָה of שַׁבָּת that has only 7 benedictions (3 + 1 + 3) is often called "שְׁמוֹנֶה עֶשְׂרֵה "

**Many philosophical and theological interpretations flow from the above.

***The prayer (in fine print) about the wind and rain is recited daily in the fall and winter.

****Source: Talmud *Taanit 7a and B'rachot 33a.*

THE THIRD OPENING BLESSING OF THE AMIDAH — קְדוּשַׁת הַשֵּׁם

God is holy (קָדוֹשׁ). The Jewish people have been charged by Moses to be a holy people (קְדוֹשִׁים). The holy people praise the Holy God.

You are holy	1. אַתָּה קָדוֹשׁ
and Your name is holy	2. וְשִׁמְךָ קָדוֹשׁ
and holy ones (i.e., Jews) — each day —	3. וּקְדוֹשִׁים — בְּכָל יוֹם —
will praise Your name.	4. יְהַלְלוּךָ, סֶלָה.
Blessed are You, O Lord,	5. בָּרוּךְ אַתָּה ה׳,
the Holy God.	6. הָאֵל הַקָּדוֹשׁ.

Our Growing Vocabulary

Comparison and Analysis	Words with a familiar ring		Words we already know		line
			You are	אַתָּה	1,5
			holy	קָדוֹשׁ	1,2,6
קָדוֹשׁ	and holy ones	וּקְדוֹשִׁים			3
בְּכָל = בְּ כָל			on every	בְּכָל	4
			day	יוֹם	4
			blessed	בָּרוּךְ	5
			God	הָאֵל	6
			the holy	הַקָּדוֹשׁ	6

Notes.

The title of this prayer is קְדוּשַׁת הַשֵּׁם (the Sanctification of the "Name"). This short prayer is recited only in the Silent עֲמִידָה. When the עֲמִידָה is repeated aloud by the cantor, the short prayer of קְדוּשַׁת הַשֵּׁם is completely supplanted by a longer prayer on the theme of holiness, namely the קְדוּשָׁה (Sanctification).

58

PROCEDURES

At public services, * in the daytime (but not at night), the Silent Devotion of the individual worshippers is traditionally followed by a Reader's Repetition ** of the עֲמִידָה. In the Repetition, the third Opening Blessing of the Amidah is replaced by the special blessing called K'dushah.***

Today, some congregations practice a modified Reader's Repetition as follows: The two Opening Blessings of the עֲמִידָה and the K'dushah are chanted aloud by the Reader and congregation; the rest of the עֲמִידָה is recited silently by the individual worshippers.****

TORAH ARK IN THE SYNAGOGUE OF ARI, OLDEST SYNAGOGUE IN SAFED, ISRAEL

*   A Public Service is created by the presence of a מִנְיָן (a quorum of 10 adults).
**   A Reader could be any qualified lay leader of the Service or a Cantor: חַזָּן=
** *   For K'dushah, see units 8 and 9.
** ** The traditional name for this modification is "a loud שְׁמוֹנֶה עֶשְׂרֵה" or "a loud קְדוּשָׁה"
See Vocabulary of Jewish life in Part II.

קְדוּשָׁה

קָדוֹשׁ קָדוֹשׁ קָדוֹשׁ

שַׁחֲרִית קְדוּשָׁה of (pp... ³⁵⁶ in your סדור)

Section I — lines 1-11.

Let us sanctify Your name throughout the world	1 נְקַדֵּשׁ אֶת שִׁמְךָ בָּעוֹלָם
as they sanctify it in the highest heavens	2 כְּשֵׁם שֶׁמַּקְדִּישִׁים אוֹתוֹ בִּשְׁמֵי מָרוֹם
As it is written by the hand of Your prophet	3 כַּכָּתוּב עַל יַד נְבִיאֶךָ
and they called one to the other and said:	4 וְקָרָא זֶה אֶל זֶה וְאָמַר:
Holy, holy, holy is the Lord of hosts**	5* קָדוֹשׁ קָדוֹשׁ קָדוֹשׁ ה' צְבָאוֹת
His glory fills all the earth.	6* מְלֹא כָל הָאָרֶץ כְּבוֹדוֹ.
	7 אָז בְּקוֹל רַעַשׁ גָּדוֹל
	8 אַדִּיר וְחָזָק מַשְׁמִיעִים קוֹל
	9 מִתְנַשְּׂאִים לְעֻמַּת שְׂרָפִים
	10 לְעֻמָּתָם בָּרוּךְ יֹאמֵרוּ:
Blessed be the glory of the Lord from His Place.	11*** בָּרוּךְ כְּבוֹד ה' מִמְּקוֹמוֹ!

Our K'dushah consists of two main sections and a brief concluding paragraph.

Section I

The key theme is, Holiness, (קְדוּשָׁה). The core word is קָדוֹשׁ (holy). Many other words are related to קָדוֹשׁ. The קְדוּשָׁה is built around two verses, one from prophet Isaiah, the other from the prophet Ezekiel.
Whereas the first section and the concluding paragraph proclaim God's holiness, the second section of קְדוּשָׁה deals with a different theme.

Notes.

* This key phrase is from Isaiah 6:3   **hosts=heavenly constellations
***From Ezekiel 3:12.
The K'dushah is built around these two verses.

<u>Section II: A new theme.</u>

12 From Your place, our King, please appear	12 מִמְּקוֹמְךָ מַלְכֵּנוּ תוֹפִיעַ
13 and reign over us	13 וְתִמְלוֹךְ עָלֵינוּ
14 For we are waiting for You.	14 כִּי מְחַכִּים אֲנַחְנוּ לָךְ.
15 (And we are asking:) When will You reign in Zion?	15 מָתַי תִּמְלוֹךְ בְּצִיוֹן?
16 Speedily in our day	16 בְּקָרוֹב בְּיָמֵינוּ
17 and forevermore may You dwell (in Zion)!	17 לְעוֹלָם וָעֶד תִּשְׁכּוֹן !
18 May Your greatness appear and may You be sanctified	18 תִּתְגַּדַּל וְתִתְקַדַּשׁ
19 in the midst of Jerusalem, Your city	19 בְּתוֹךְ יְרוּשָׁלַיִם עִירְךָ
20 throughout all generations	20 לְדוֹר וָדוֹר
21 and throughout all eternities	21 וּלְנֵצַח נְצָחִים
22 and may our eyes (be privileged to) see Your Kingship,	22 וְעֵינֵינוּ תִרְאֶינָה מַלְכוּתֶךָ
23 according to the word spoken in Your majestic psalms by David, Your righteously Anointed:	23 כַּדָּבָר הָאָמוּר בְּשִׁירֵי עֻזֶּךָ עַל־יְדֵי דָוִד מְשִׁיחַ צִדְקֶךָ
24 May the Lord reign forever!	24 יִמְלוֹךְ ה׳ לְעוֹלָם
25 Your God, O Zion (shall reign) unto all generations!	25 אֱלֹהַיִךְ צִיּוֹן, לְדוֹר וָדוֹר !
26 Praised be the Lord!	26 הַלְלוּיָהּ !

Notes.

The themes of Section I and Section II of קְדוּשָׁה are different.
The first section of קְדוּשָׁה ends with the word מִמְּקוֹמוֹ (from His place) — line 11
The second part of קְדוּשָׁה of שַׁחֲרִית begins with the word מִמְּקוֹמְךָ (from Your place) — line 12
The word מִמְּקוֹמוֹ marks the transition to Section II.
The theme of Section II is Zion.

62

Comparison and Analysis	New words	Words with a familiar ring	Words we already know	line
name שֵׁם		Your name שִׁמְךָ		1
בָּעוֹלָם = בָּ עוֹלָם			in the world בָּעוֹלָם	1
			קָדוֹשׁ קָדוֹשׁ קָדוֹשׁ Holy, holy, holy	5
			the Lord ה'	5,11
			the earth הָאָרֶץ	6
			blessed be בָּרוּךְ	11
			the glory of כְּבוֹד	11
place מָקוֹם	from his place מִמְּקוֹמוֹ			11
			our King מַלְכֵּנוּ	12
			upon us עָלֵינוּ	13
		in Zion בְּצִיּוֹן		15
	When? מָתַי		forever	15
			and ever לְעוֹלָם וָעֶד	17
		Jerusalem יְרוּשָׁלַיִם		19
	unto all generations לְדוֹר וָדוֹר			20,25
		Messiah מָשִׁיחַ		23
		David דָּוִד		23
			forever לְעוֹלָם	24
			Lord ה'	24
		Zion צִיּוֹן		25
Your God אֱלֹהֶיךָ		Your God אֱלֹהַיִךְ		25
		Praise the Lord הַלְלוּיָהּ		26

SECTION I

שַׁחֲרִית of קְדוּשָׁה

The evidence of God's glory is throughout the Universe.
God is One. His works are manifold, all around you, above you, in you.
The heavens, the wondersome constellations, the "angelic beings" — declare His holiness.
"Where is God's glory? It fills the Universe."

Holiness, Glory and Place.

The prophets were overwhelmed by the glory of the Universe and by the ineffable glory and holiness of the Creator who is in the Universe and beyond the Universe.
They spoke of God's Place and Presence even as they were overwhelmed by the sense of His Omnipresence.

מוּסָף of קְדוּשָׁה (See Unit 9)

In the prophetic vision even the angels find it hard to pinpoint — "Where is God?"
His glory fills the Universe.
Their final answer is puzzling; what do they say?
Here is how some Sages of the Talmud put it: The name of God is Place (מָקוֹם)
The world is not the place of God. God is the place of the world. The world is in God.*

*Source: Midrash, Breshit Rabbah, chapter 68. See also Seligman Baer — *Seder Avodat Yisrael* p. 237.

The ideas.
_____
Yearnings for Zion

Section II of קְדוּשָׁה speaks of Zion.

The Jewish prayerbook speaks of Zion, continually, in many places.

The prayerbook has proclaimed Jerusalem, the city of our people, the capital of the Jewish land, forever. The prayerbook has been a source of hopes and yearnings for Zion throughout all the generations of exile.

Where? God's special place — in Zion

Section I of קְדוּשָׁה ends with the word " מִמְּקוֹמוֹ " = "from His Place."

That word triggered in the heart of the Jew a plea, beginning with these words: "From Your Place (מִמְּקוֹמְךָ) please appear, O Lord, and reign over us in Zion for we are waiting for You."

Yes, God is everywhere. Yet the Jew always felt that God's presence was especially pervasive in one sacred spot: in Zion, in Jerusalem, because God has chosen Zion.

When?

Ever since the beginning of the Exile the Jew has been asking: When will You, O Lord, appear from Your Cosmic Place and make Your Kingship evident in Zion?

We are waiting!

Empires fall, centuries pass. The Jew still waits. Pleadingly he asks:

How long? When? When will you reign again in Zion?

Do proclaim Your greatness and Your holiness in the midst of Jerusalem, Your city, speedily in our day.

Make it forever; for all generations; for all eternity.

May our eyes behold Your Kingship — as envisioned by the Psalms of David —

"Your God, O Zion, shall reign forever and ever."

TIME AND ETERNITY CONSCIOUS

The Jew has always been time and eternity conscious. Both history and destiny have been built into Jewish prayers. The "time phrases" of קְדוּשָׁה are an expression of both memory and hope.

Forever and ever	לְעוֹלָם וָעֶד	When?	מָתַי ?
throughout all generations	לְדוֹר וָדוֹר	Speedily, in our days	בְּקָרוֹב בְּיָמֵינוּ
throughout all eternities	לְנֶצַח נְצָחִים		

In the final section...

In the short final section of קְדוּשָׁה we find a full roster of both "time phrases" and "holiness phrases"

לְדוֹר וָדוֹר נַגִּיד גָּדְלֶךָ . וּלְנֵצַח נְצָחִים קְדֻשָּׁתְךָ נַקְדִּישׁ.
> Unto all generations we will declare Your greatness. Throughout all eternity we will sanctify Your holiness.

וְשִׁבְחֲךָ אֱלֹהֵינוּ מִפִּינוּ לֹא יָמוּשׁ לְעוֹלָם וָעֶד. כִּי אֵל
> Your praise, our God, shall never cease from our mouth.

מֶלֶךְ גָּדוֹל וְקָדוֹשׁ אָתָּה. בָּרוּךְ אַתָּה יְיָ הָאֵל הַקָּדוֹשׁ:
> You are indeed a great and holy God. Blessed are You, O Lord, the holy God.

Procedure.

During the Repetition of the עֲמִידָה the "holiness prayer" of קְדוּשָׁה completely supplants the short third Opening Blessing known as קְדוּשַׁת הַשֵּׁם.

On Shabbat, holiday and Rosh Hodesh mornings we have two קְדוּשׁוֹת :

One for the שַׁחֲרִית of עֲמִידָה and a different one for the עֲמִידָה of מוּסָף

This unit deals with the קְדוּשָׁה of שַׁחֲרִית. Unit 9 will deal with the קְדוּשָׁה of מוּסָף.

The concluding paragraph is chanted by cantor. The two main sections are chanted responsively by congregation and cantor (in that order).

A moment of solemnity.

Everybody stands "at attention" during קְדוּשָׁה. No one walks or talks during קְדוּשָׁה.

Anyone entering the synagogue at this point remains standing at the door and is permitted to move only after the recital of קְדוּשָׁה is completed.

See Vocabulary of Jewish Life in Part II of book.

The upper part of the memorial at the Park
Avenue Synagogue in New York City. Sculptor,
Nathan Rapoport.

וְהוּא יַשְׁמִיעֵנוּ בְּרַחֲמָיו, שֵׁנִית לְעֵינֵי כָּל חַי

סִדּוּר) מוּסָף of מוּסָף קְדוּשָׁה (pp..... in your

SECTION I

| (Compared with K'dushah of שַׁחֲרִית) | K'dushah of מוּסָף |

K'dushah of מוּסָף

		מוּסָף column (right)
1		נַעֲרִיצְךָ וְנַקְדִּישְׁךָ כְּסוֹד שִׂיחַ שַׂרְפֵי קֹדֶשׁ
2		הַמַּקְדִּישִׁים שִׁמְךָ בַּקּוֹדֶשׁ
3		כַּכָּתוּב עַל יַד נְבִיאֶךָ
4		וְקָרָא זֶה אֶל זֶה וְאָמַר:
5	Holy holy holy is the Lord of hosts	קָדוֹשׁ קָדוֹשׁ קָדוֹשׁ ה׳ צְבָאוֹת
6	His glory fills all the earth	מְלֹא כָל הָאָרֶץ כְּבוֹדוֹ
7	The Universe is full of His glory	כְּבוֹדוֹ מָלֵא עוֹלָם
8	His ministering angels ask one another:	מְשָׁרְתָיו שׁוֹאֲלִים זֶה לָזֶה:
9	Where is the place of His glory?	אַיֵּה מְקוֹם כְּבוֹדוֹ؟
10	They respond to one another:	לְעוּמָתָם בָּרוּךְ יֹאמֵרוּ:
11	Blessed be the glory of the Lord from His Place.	בָּרוּךְ כְּבוֹד ה׳ מִמְּקוֹמוֹ !

שַׁחֲרִית column (left):

1 נְקַדֵּשׁ אֶת שִׁמְךָ בָּעוֹלָם
2 כְּשֵׁם שֶׁמַּקְדִּישִׁים אוֹתוֹ בִּשְׁמֵי מָרוֹם
3 כַּכָּתוּב עַל יַד נְבִיאֶךָ
4 וְקָרָא זֶה אֶל זֶה וְאָמַר:
5 קָדוֹשׁ קָדוֹשׁ קָדוֹשׁ ה׳ צְבָאוֹת
6 מְלֹא כָל הָאָרֶץ כְּבוֹדוֹ
7 אָז בְּקוֹל רַעַשׁ גָּדוֹל
8 אַדִּיר וְחָזָק מַשְׁמִיעִים קוֹל

מִתְנַשְּׂאִים לְעוּמַת שְׂרָפִים
לְעוּמָתָם בָּרוּךְ יֹאמְרוּ:
בָּרוּךְ כְּבוֹד ה׳ מִמְּקוֹמוֹ !

Notes.

The קְדוּשָׁה of מוּסָף like the קְדוּשָׁה of שַׁחֲרִית consists of two main sections and a brief concluding paragraph. The concluding paragraph deals with God's holiness and is completely identical with the corresponding paragraph in the קְדוּשָׁה of שַׁחֲרִית.

The first section also deals with holiness like its counterpart in שַׁחֲרִית; yet while the content is similar it is not fully identical.

The theme is holiness. The key verses from Isaiah 6 and Ezekiel 3 are the same as in the K'dushah of שַׁחֲרִית. In fact lines 3-6 and 10-11 are identical.

The other lines use different words but the underlying ideas are similar.

12 From His Place may He turn in mercy	מִמְּקוֹמוֹ הוּא יִפֶן בְּרַחֲמִים	12
13 And bestow grace upon a people who proclaim the unity of His Name.	וְיָחוֹן עַם הַמְּיַחֲדִים שְׁמוֹ	13
14 Evening and morning of each day, perpetually,	עֶרֶב וָבוֹקֶר בְּכָל יוֹם תָּמִיד	14
15 Twice, in love, they say Sh'ma:	פַּעֲמַיִם בְּאַהֲבָה שְׁמַע אוֹמְרִים	15
16 "Hear O Israel, the Lord our God, the Lord is One"	"שְׁמַע יִשְׂרָאֵל ה' אֱלֹהֵינוּ ה' אֶחָד"	16
17 He is our God. He is our Father.	הוּא אֱלֹהֵינוּ, הוּא אָבִינוּ	17
18 He is our King. He is our Deliverer.	הוּא מַלְכֵּנוּ, הוּא מוֹשִׁיעֵנוּ	18
19 May He in His mercy make us hear, for a second time,	וְהוּא יַשְׁמִיעֵנוּ בְּרַחֲמָיו, שֵׁנִית	19
20 In the presence (literally: "before the eyes" of all the living:	לְעֵינֵי כָּל חַי	20
21 "...in order to be your God.	"לִהְיוֹת לָכֶם לֵאלֹהִים	21
22 I am the Lord your God."	אֲנִי ה' אֱלֹהֵיכֶם"	22
23 As it is written in Your holy Scripture,	וּבְדִבְרֵי קָדְשְׁךָ כָּתוּב לֵאמֹר	23
24 May the Lord reign forever!	יִמְלֹךְ ה' לְעוֹלָם !	24
25 Your God, O Zion, (shall reign) unto all generations!	אֱלֹהַיִךְ צִיּוֹן, לְדוֹר וָדוֹר !	25
26 Give praise to the Lord!	הַלְלוּיָהּ !	26

Notes.

═══════════

The קְדוּשָׁה of מוּסָף like its counterpart the קְדוּשָׁה of שַׁחֲרִית develops in its second section a theme other then holiness.

The first part of קְדוּשָׁה ends with the word מִמְּקוֹמוֹ (=from His place) — line 11.

The second part of the קְדוּשָׁה of מוּסָף begins with the word מִמְּקוֹמוֹ (=from His place) — line 12.

This word מִמְּקוֹמוֹ constitutes the link between the two parts.

The theme of Section II of the קְדוּשָׁה of מוּסָף is the pronouncement of שְׁמַע

lines 24-26 are fully identical with lines 24-26 in the קְדוּשָׁה of שַׁחֲרִית (see p...)

The Concluding Paragraph of קְדוּשָׁה is the same as in קְדוּשָׁה of שַׁחֲרִית (see p...)

Comparison and and Analysis		New Words		Words with familiar ring		Words we already know		line
						holy	קָדוֹשׁ	5
						the Lord	ה׳	5,11
						all	כָּל	6
						the earth	הָאָרֶץ	6
						universe	עוֹלָם	7
		where	אַיֵּה					9
place	מָקוֹם			the place of	מְקוֹם			9
						blessed be	בָּרוּך	10,11
						the glory of...	כְּבוֹד	11
place	מָקוֹם					from his place	מִמְּקוֹמוֹ	11

70

Comparison and Analysis	New Words	Words with a familiar ring	Words we already know		line
			He	הוּא	12
בְּ רַחֲמִים			in mercy	בְּרַחֲמִים	12
			a people	עַם	13
בְּ כָּל			on every	בְּכָל	14
			day	יוֹם	14
			hear	שְׁמַע	16
			Israel	יִשְׂרָאֵל	16
			the Lord	ה׳	16,22,24
אֱלֹהִים			our God	אֱלֹהֵינוּ	16
			one	אֶחָד	16
			he is	הוּא	17,18
אֱלֹהִים			our God	אֱלֹהֵינוּ	17
אָבִינוּ מַלְכֵּנוּ			our father	אָבִינוּ	17
מֶלֶךְ			our King	מַלְכֵּנוּ	18
מוֹשִׁיעַ			our deliverer	מוֹשִׁיעֵנוּ	18
וְ הוּא			and he	וְהוּא	19
			all	כָּל	20
אֱלֹהִים		unto God	לֵאלֹהִים		21
אֱלֹהֶיךָ		your God (plural)	אֱלֹהֵיכֶם		22
			forever	לְעוֹלָם	24
			your God	אֱלֹהַיִךְ	25
			Zion	צִיּוֹן	25
				לְדוֹר וָדוֹר	25
			throughout the generations		
			Praise the Lord	הַלְלוּיָהּ	26

A confrontation with history.

We reread p. 69 lines 12-16 (in English and Hebrew)! and we are puzzled: What is the שְׁמַע doing in the קְדוּשָׁה prayer and what is the meaning of the fervent plea contained in these lines? The answer is:

We are in a confrontation with history, with one of the recurrent chapters of "persecution and response." The Jewish idea of "One God" irritated megalomaniacal emperors and the priests of pagan polytheism, Zoroastrian dualism and Christian trinitarianism throughout the ages. The assertion of שְׁמַע was perceived as a threatening challenge to their beliefs and they forbade it under penalty of death. The Jewish response: stubborn assertion through evasion. Since spies were sent into the synagogues to make sure the government edict was obeyed, the Jews stopped reciting the שְׁמַע early in the service at the halachically prescribed time. However when the spies departed, the key passage of שְׁמַע turned up as a defiant proclamation and a poignant plea at a later part of the service, namely in the קְדוּשָׁה of מוּסָף. *

Upon hearing the cherished (and forbidden) words of the שְׁמַע (line 16) the Jewish congregation would burst out with defiant enthusiasm:

He is (indeed) our God, He is our Father! He is our King, He is our Redeemer! (lines 17-18 of קְדוּשָׁה)

הוּא אֱלֹהֵינוּ, הוּא אָבִינוּ, הוּא מַלְכֵּנוּ, הוּא מוֹשִׁיעֵנוּ

First the Jews pleaded to God to ackownledge their loyalty ("Turn in mercy and extend Your grace to the people who proclaim God's unity, in love, perpetually") under all kinds of trying circumstances (lines 12-16).
Then came the next plea: (lines 19-22)

19 May God in His mercy make us hear for a second time	19 וְהוּא יַשְׁמִיעֵנוּ בְּרַחֲמָיו שֵׁנִית
20 before the eyes of all the living:	20 לְעֵינֵי כָּל חַי
21 "...in order to be your God.	21 לִהְיוֹת לָכֶם לֵאלֹהִים
22 I am the Lord your God."	22 אֲנִי ה׳ אֱלֹהֵיכֶם

Lines 21-22 (in the "box") quote the last six words of שְׁמַע
Line 16 (in "box" on p69) contains the first six words of שְׁמַע
Together lines 16 and 21-22 represent the entire שְׁמַע
The oppressed generations pleaded to God: Proclaim (= "Make us hear") these words of שְׁמַע for a second time (line 19).
When did we hear them for the first time? After the liberation from Egypt.
They prayed: May we hear these words again for a second time publicly and loudly after the new liberation from this current oppression; before the eyes of all the living; for all the world to hear and see.

*What are the historic dates of those events? Theories differ. According to Dr. Louis Finkelstein — in the days of the pagan Roman Emperor Hadrian of Rabbi Akiba's time.   According to others — in the day of Isdagir II, the King of Persia, of the 5th century who viewed the שְׁמַע as a threat against his dualistic theology of Zoroastrianism.

FOR YOUR ENRICHMENT

שַׁחֲרִית of קְדוּשָׁה

Theme: Place מָקוֹם	Theme: Glory כָּבוֹד	Theme: Holiness קָדֵשׁ
	1 מְלֹא כָל הָאָרֶץ כְּבוֹדוֹ	נְקַדֵּשׁ אֶת שִׁמְךָ בָּעוֹלָם
בָּרוּךְ כְּבוֹד ה׳ מִמְּקוֹמוֹ	2 כְּשֵׁם שֶׁמַּקְדִּישִׁים אוֹתוֹ בִּשְׁמֵי מָרוֹם בָּרוּךְ כְּבוֹד ה׳ מִמְּקוֹמוֹ	
	3 קָדוֹשׁ קָדוֹשׁ קָדוֹשׁ ה׳ צְבָאוֹת	

מוּסָף of קְדוּשָׁה

Theme: Place = מָקוֹם	Theme: Glory = כָּבוֹד	Theme: Holiness = קָדֵשׁ
אַיֵּה מְקוֹם כְּבוֹדוֹ	מְלֹא כָל הָאָרֶץ כְּבוֹדוֹ	נַעֲרִיצְךָ וְנַקְדִּישְׁךָ כְּסוֹד שִׂיחַ
בָּרוּךְ כְּבוֹד ה׳ מִמְּקוֹמוֹ	כְּבוֹדוֹ מָלֵא עוֹלָם	שַׂרְפֵי קֹדֶשׁ
	אַיֵּה מְקוֹם כְּבוֹדוֹ	הַמַּקְדִּישִׁים שִׁמְךָ בַּקֹּדֶשׁ
	בָּרוּךְ כְּבוֹד ה׳ מִמְּקוֹמוֹ	קָדוֹשׁ קָדוֹשׁ קָדוֹשׁ ה׳ צְבָאוֹת

Procedures

The synagogue procedures and the responsive chanting are the same as for the קְדוּשָׁה of שַׁחֲרִית.

See Vocabulary of Jewish Life in Part II of this book

קָדוּשׁ and וְשָׁמְרוּ of Shabbat morning

Unit 10a.: The Shabbat — An Eternal Covenant

God has made a Covenant with the Children of Israel, and has given them the Shabbat as a sign of the Covenant.

Unit 10.b   קָדוּשׁ is the Jew's proclamation of the holiness of שַׁבָּת

KIDDUSH CUP (from Frankfort Synagogue)
Frankfort—on—the— Main, Germany, 1600. Gold

AND THEY SHALL KEEP וְשָׁמְרוּ

Unit 10a

1 And the children of Israel shall keep the Sabbath	1 וְשָׁמְרוּ בְנֵי יִשְׂרָאֵל אֶת הַשַּׁבָּת
2 to make the Sabbath	2 לַעֲשׂוֹת אֶת הַשַּׁבָּת
3 throughout their generations	3 לְדֹרוֹתָם
4 as an everlasting Covenant.	4 בְּרִית עוֹלָם
5 Between me and between the children of Israel —	— 5 בֵּינִי וּבֵין בְּנֵי יִשְׂרָאֵל
6 it is a sign forever	6 אוֹת הִיא לְעוֹלָם
7 that in six days God made heaven and earth	7 כִּי שֵׁשֶׁת יָמִים עָשָׂה ה׳ אֶת הַשָּׁמַיִם וְאֶת הָאָרֶץ
8 And on the seventh day He ceased from work and was refreshed.	8 וּבַיוֹם הַשְּׁבִיעִי שָׁבַת—וַיִּנָּפַשׁ

Notes.

The biblical passage וְשָׁמְרוּ (Exodus 31:16-I7) is used in the Shabbat services on 3 occasions.
a) just before the עֲמִידָה on Friday night. (p.... in your סִדּוּר)
b) as part of the עֲמִידָה of שַׁחֲרִית on Shabbat morning (p..... in your סִדּוּר)
c) as an optional introductory part of the קִדּוּשׁ of Shabbat morning.*

Some meanings behind the text

Line 1 — וְשָׁמְרוּ... אֶת הַשַּׁבָּת — "and they shall keep the Sabbath" gave birth to the concept of
שׁוֹמֵר שַׁבָּת = Keeper of the Sabbath.
Line 2 — "to make the Sabbath" is a literal and most accurate translation of לַעֲשׂוֹת אֶת הַשַּׁבָּת
Through the usual rendition "to observe the Sabbath" the essence of this sentence gets lost in translation.
*Line 4 — בְּרִית is a Covenant. בְּרִית מִילָה — is the Covenant of circumcision. בְּנֵי בְּרִית — means "Sons of the Covenant."
Line 8 — וַיִּנָּפַשׁ = "and He was refreshed." Most renditions translate "and he rested".

Comparison and Analysis	New Words	Words with a familiar sound	Words we already know	line
			Sabbath שַׁבָּת	1,2
			Israel יִשְׂרָאֵל	1,5
			The children of Israel בְּנֵי יִשְׂרָאֵל	1,5
בְּרִית מִילָה בְּנֵי בְּרִית בְּרִית עוֹלָם an eternal covenant		covenant בְּרִית		4
			eternity עוֹלָם	4
			forever לְעוֹלָם	6
			the Lord ה׳	7
			the heavens הַשָּׁמַיִם	7
			the earth הָאָרֶץ	7
וּבַיוֹם=וּ בַ יוֹם		and on the day וּבַיוֹם		8
Seventh Aliyah שְׁבִיעִי		the seventh הַשְּׁבִיעִי		8

76

The ideas
The Shabbat — A major contribution to civilization

The name "Sabbath" was adopted, with a slight change, from the Hebrew Shabbat (שַׁבָּת).
A weekly day of rest has been a major contribution of Judaism to human civilization.
Weeks and months are not chains of endless toil.
One day out of seven a person is given an opportunity to stop:
Catch your breath, refresh yourself, rest, think, meditate, look back, look forward, reunite with family, read, study, sleep!

And they shall keep   =   וְשָׁמְרוּ (line 1)

One of the key rationales for the observance of שַׁבָּת is provided in our biblical passage which has been incorporated into three of our Shabbat services.
"To keep the Shabbat" has become the technical term which describes the "doing" of a number of "Shabbasdik" things and refraining from many "non-Shabbasdik" things, that collectively add up to the creation of the special spirit of the day.
From the word " וְשָׁמְרוּ " (= "and they shall keep") comes the term " שׁוֹמֵר שַׁבָּת " (= the one who keeps the שַׁבָּת).
In the past almost every Jew was a שׁוֹמֵר שַׁבָּת.

To make the Shabbat   =   לַעֲשׂוֹת אֶת הַשַׁבָּת (line 2)

A very significant message is encapsuled in the literal text. The children of Israel have been commanded "to make the Sabbath." You have to prepare for it. You have to create the atmosphere. In Yiddish it is called "Machen Shabbes."
There is no Sabbath unless you make it. You have to make it happen.
By the calendar Friday Night and Saturday morning do not look different or feel different from a Monday or a Wednesday. However, the Jews, the children of Israel, make the Shabbat into a special day.
The family together, the washed faces of the children, the Shabbat dress, the candlelighting, the Kiddush, the wine, the Hallah, the "gefillte fish," the chicken soup, the table songs (Z'mirot), the exclusion of all the physical pressures of the outside world, the going to the synagogue together, Torah study — they make the Shabbat. The Jew was always aware that: God created the first שַׁבָּת; but the Jew recreates the Shabbat every seventh day.

שַׁבָּת is portable

Wherever Jews "make שַׁבָּת " there is שַׁבָּת.
Wherever Jews live, anywhere in the world, and they wish to remember the Covenant, there is a Shabbat.
Where the Shabbat is forgotten the Covenant is broken.

A Covenant forever: An Eternal Covenant בְּרִית עוֹלָם (line 4)

The "making" of Shabbat is part of the covenant between God and the children of Israel.
Normal treaties are not lasting; most treaties are broken at some point.
A covenant is a solemn treaty, meant to last.
God made a covenant, a solemn treaty, with the children of Israel (line 5) which is not limited to any one place or to any one time.
God's covenant with the children of Israel is both universal and eternal. לְעוֹלָם — line 6.
It is inherited, continued, and renewed throughout the generations. לְדוֹרוֹתָם — line 3.

And on the seventh day he ceased working שָׁבַת (line 8)

The Bible tells us that work and creativity are not an uninterrupted perpetual progression and that periods of work must be followed by periods of "cessation from work." The Hebrew verb that means "He ceased from work" שָׁבַת is at the root of the Hebrew noun שַׁבָּת, which means "a Day of cessation from work."
The primary function of שַׁבָּת is "cessation from work." However, two things should be understood:
1) "Work" in the biblical and Talmudic understanding means not only hard menial labor but any effort that changes the physical world around us. e.g. cooking, writing, sewing, etc.
   2) To cease from work alone is not enough. There has to be something more, as we shall see below.

And He was refreshed וַיִּנָּפַשׁ (line 8)

וַיִּנָּפַשׁ at the end of line 8 of וְשָׁמְרוּ is rendered in most English translations as "and He rested." Our translation, following the new Torah translation (JPS 1962, p. 157), renders it: "and He was refreshed." Why? Because the Hebrew verb וַיִּנָּפַשׁ is a very rare word. It occurs in the entire Bible only three times and is related to the Hebrew words for soul and for breathing. (נֶפֶשׁ)
The closest translation would be: "He caught up with His soul!" or "He caught His breath" or "He restored His soul."
What a magnificent image — God catching up with His soul.

The world needs to catch up with its soul

We know today that:
Mineral resources, forests, water, air — and even ozone layers — are not inexhaustible.
Man is not inexhaustible.
The soil which is farmed needs a rest.
The whole world needs to catch its breath from time to time.
Conclusion: Jews must keep the Sabbath as a reminder forever that the world needs to catch up with its soul.

THE SHABBAT MORNING KIDDUSH

The Kiddush of Shabbat morning consists of one standard version and two optional introductions.

I. Introduction — optional

The standard version of the Shabbat morning Kiddush is very brief (see right column)
That is all that is required. However,
many people also chant an introductory part which is optional.
The introduction comes in two alternative versions:
(1) The more popular alternative is our text of וְשָׁמְרוּ

וְשָׁמְרוּ בְנֵי יִשְׂרָאֵל אֶת הַשַּׁבָּת
לַעֲשׂוֹת אֶת הַשַּׁבָּת לְדֹרוֹתָם
בְּרִית עוֹלָם
בֵּינִי וּבֵין בְּנֵי יִשְׂרָאֵל — אוֹת הִיא לְעוֹלָם
כִּי שֵׁשֶׁת יָמִים עָשָׂה ה' אֶת הַשָּׁמַיִם וְאֶת הָאָרֶץ
וּבַיּוֹם הַשְּׁבִיעִי שָׁבַת — וַיִּנָּפַשׁ

(2) Another less frequently used alternative are the three sentences of the 4th of the Ten Commandments — the Sabbath Commandment (Exodus 20:8-11).
Notes.

II. Standard format — required

The required format of the Shabbat morning קִדּוּשׁ is the following:

a. (Sanctification)

עַל כֵּן בֵּרַךְ ה' אֶת יוֹם הַשַּׁבָּת וַיְקַדְּשֵׁהוּ.

"and therefore G/d blessed the Sabbath Day and made it holy" (Exodus 20:11)
b. (Courtesy formula)

סַבְרִי מָרָנָן וְרַבָּנָן וְרַבּוֹתַי

"With the permission of all of you,
my masters and teachers"

c. בָּרוּךְ אַתָּה ה' אֱלֹהֵינוּ מֶלֶךְ הָעוֹלָם בּוֹרֵא פְּרִי הַגָּפֶן.

"Praised be You, O Lord our God, King of the Universe who creates the fruit of the vine."

שַׁבָּת in Jewish tradition was always referred to as שַׁבָּת קֹדֶשׁ — a Sabbath of holiness.
קִדּוּשׁ = means sanctification=The Proclamation of the Holiness of שַׁבָּת.

   Item "a" comprises the sanctification formula (קִדּוּשׁ). It is the last part of the third sentence of the 4th Commandment (Exodus 20:11).
   The wine blessing by itself (item c) does not constitute Kiddush.
Most Jewish people know the wine blessing by heart. In many congregations they also sing וְשָׁמְרוּ by heart.

Our growing vocabulary

Comparison and Analysis	New words		Words with a familiar ring		Words we already know	
בָּרוּךְ	he blessed	בֵּרַךְ			the Lord	ה'
קָדוֹשׁ	and he sanctified it	וַיְקַדְּשֵׁהוּ				
			who creates	בּוֹרֵא	blessed	בָּרוּךְ
			fruit of...	פְּרִי	are You	אַתָּה
			the vine	הַגָּפֶן	Lord	ה'
					Our G—d	אֱלֹהֵינוּ
					King of...	מֶלֶךְ
					the Universe	הָעוֹלָם

PROCEDURES

1. The essence of קִדּוּשׁ is the sanctification of the שַׁבָּת. As part of the ritual of Sanctification we use wine to honor the שַׁבָּת. While "בּוֹרֵא פְּרִי הַגָּפֶן" as the blessing over the wine is an ingredient of the קִדּוּשׁ it is not קִדּוּשׁ in its own rights.

2. קִדּוּשׁ is recited both in the synagogue and in the home.

   a) The more important of the two is the קִדּוּשׁ in the house. Kiddush is the required introduction to the meal of שַׁבָּת. One is not supposed to eat before the קִדּוּשׁ has been recited. The Kiddush can be recited by one person on behalf of everyone; those present get a sip of wine. The קִדּוּשׁ is followed by the "Hamotzi" blessing over the חַלָה*(Prior to making the הַמּוֹצִיא you wash your hands.)

   b) The קִדּוּשׁ at the synagogue on Saturday morning is recited after the conclusion of the services.

*The blessing over Hallah (or over any bread) is: בָּרוּךְ אַתָּה ה' אֱלֹהֵינוּ מֶלֶךְ הָעוֹלָם הַמּוֹצִיא לֶחֶם מִן הָאָרֶץ
(= "Blessed are You, O Lord, our God, King of the Universe, who brings forth bread from the soil").

See Vocabulary of Jewish life in Part II

TWO SHABBAT PRAYERS:

יִשְׂמְחוּ   רְצֵה בִּמְנוּחָתֵנוּ

Shabbat in the Jewish home

The day of Shabbat in authentic Jewish life is a day for the spiritual self, for family togetherness, for contemplation, study, and discussion; and for an uplifting rest in the afternoon. For pious souls it is also a time for spiritual ecstasy.

REST!   *REFLECT!*   *REJOICE!*

A. MAY THEY REJOICE IN YOUR KINGSHIP יִשְׂמְחוּ

(p..... in your prayerbook in the Amidah of מוּסָף)

1 May they who rejoice in Your Kingship   יִשְׂמְחוּ בְמַלְכוּתְךָ .1

2 those who observe the Sabbath and call it a delight;   שׁוֹמְרֵי שַׁבָּת וְקוֹרְאֵי עֹנֶג .2

3 the people who sanctify the seventh day   עַם מְקַדְּשֵׁי שְׁבִיעִי .3

4 may, all of them be satisfied and delighted with Your bounty   כֻּלָּם יִשְׂבְּעוּ וְיִתְעַנְּגוּ מִטּוּבֶךָ .4

5 The seventh day: You have favored it and sanctified it;   וְהַשְּׁבִיעִי רָצִיתָ בּוֹ וְקִדַּשְׁתּוֹ .5

6 You have called it the most desirable of days   חֶמְדַּת יָמִים אוֹתוֹ קָרָאתָ .6

7 in remembrance of the works of the Beginning (= Creation)   זֵכֶר לְמַעֲשֵׂה בְרֵאשִׁית .7

B: FIND FAVOR IN OUR REST רְצֵה בִמְנוּחָתֵנוּ

(p..... in your prayerbook, both in מוּסָף and שַׁחֲרִית)

8 Our God and God of our fathers   אֱלֹהֵינוּ וֵאלֹהֵי אֲבוֹתֵינוּ 8

9 accept (= favor) our rest   רְצֵה בִמְנוּחָתֵנוּ 9

10 Make us holy with Your commandments   קַדְּשֵׁנוּ בְּמִצְוֹתֶיךָ 10

11 and give us a portion in Your Torah   וְתֵן חֶלְקֵנוּ בְּתוֹרָתֶךָ 11

12 Satisfy us with Your bounty   שַׂבְּעֵנוּ מִטּוּבֶךָ 12

13 make us rejoice in Your salvation   וְשַׂמְּחֵנוּ בִּישׁוּעָתֶךָ 13

14 and purify our heart — to serve You in truth.   וְטַהֵר לִבֵּנוּ — לְעָבְדְּךָ בֶּאֱמֶת. 14

15 Let us inherit O Lord our God —   וְהַנְחִילֵנוּ — ה' אֱלֹהֵינוּ 15

16 — in love and favor — Your holy Sabbath   בְּאַהֲבָה וּבְרָצוֹן — שַׁבַּת קָדְשֶׁךָ 16

17 and may the people of Israel, who sanctify Your name, rest thereon.   וְיָנוּחוּ בוֹ יִשְׂרָאֵל מְקַדְּשֵׁי שְׁמֶךָ 17

18 Praised be You, O Lord, who sanctifies the Sabbath.   בָּרוּךְ אַתָּה ה' מְקַדֵּשׁ הַשַּׁבָּת 18

Notes.

רְצֵה בִמְנוּחָתֵנוּ appears in the Sabbath prayers five times:
1) Friday Night, p..... in your prayerbook
2) Friday Night, p..... in your prayerbook
3) In שַׁחֲרִית, p..... in your prayerbook
4) מוּסָף, p..... in your prayerbook
5) מִנְחָה, p..... in your prayerbook.

The Prayers of this Unit

The Jew here speaks not about God, but to God. He is asking for something. He speaks of individual needs and satisfactions; he speaks of joy, of rest, of integrity, and of togetherness. Even so, the individual worshipper still uses the plural "us" and "our."
He is involved with all the other Jews in the exaltation and delight of שַׁבָּת

We are not speaking here about God.

We are speaking to God (Your=ךְ...)

We are all in it together.

I speak not only for myself,
but for all of us

With Your commandments	בְּמִצְוֹתֶיךָ 10	Make us holy	קַדְּשֵׁנוּ 10	Our God	אֱלֹהֵינוּ 8	
In Your Torah	בְּתוֹרָתֶךָ 11	Satisfy us	שַׂבְּעֵנוּ 12	Our Fathers	אֲבוֹתֵינוּ 8	
From (with) Your bounty	מִטּוּבֶךָ 12	Make us rejoice	שַׂמְּחֵנוּ 13	In our rest	בִמְנוּחָתֵנוּ 9	
In Your deliverance	בִּישׁוּעָתֶךָ 13	Let us inherit	הַנְחִילֵנוּ 15	Our portion	חֶלְקֵנוּ 11	
To serve You	לְעָבְדְךָ 14			Our heart	לִבֵּנוּ 14	
Your holy Sabbath	שַׁבַּת קָדְשֶׁךָ 16					
Your name	שְׁמֶךָ 17					

נוּ = us (when attached to a verb) נוּ = our (when attached to a noun)

83

Comparison and Analysis	New words		Words which have familiar ring		Words that we already know		line
עוֹנֶג שַׁבָּת	Delight	עוֹנֶג				יִשְׂמְחוּ	2
					שַׁבָּת	Sabbath	2
עַם יִשְׂרָאֵל חַי					עַם	people; nation	3
7th Aliyah שְׁבִיעִי			שְׁבִיעִי	Seventh			3
וְהַשְׁבִיעִי = וְ הַ שְׁבִיעִי			וְהַשְׁבִיעִי				5
				and the seventh			
day יוֹם			יָמִים	days			
			בְּרֵאשִׁית	Genesis; days of Creation			7
							רְצֵה בִמְנוּחָתֵנוּ
					אֱלֹהֵינוּ	Our God	1
					וֵאלֹהֵי	and the God of..	1
					אֲבוֹתֵינוּ	our fathers	1
					בֶּאֱמֶת	the truth	14
					ה׳	the Lord	15
					אֱלֹהֵינוּ	our God	15
			בְּאַהֲבָה	in love			16
					יִשְׂרָאֵל	Israel	17
					בָּרוּךְ	blessed	18
					אַתָּה	You; are you	18
					ה׳	Lord	18
			מְקַדֵּשׁ	who sanctifies			18
					הַשַּׁבָּת	the Shabbat	18

84

The ideas

שַׁבָּת — A Special Treasure.

Love; Inheritance וְהַנְחִילֵנוּ בְּאַהֲבָה וּבְרָצוֹן

God said to Moses, I have a precious jewel in my treasure trove. It is called " שַׁבָּת " I shall give it to the children of Israel. Let them cherish it and keep it.*

The Shabbat treasure given to the Israelites as an act of love has indeed enriched the lives of our people and has been handed down from parents to children as a most precious heritage.

Every time we recite the Kiddush, we become aware again that God made us inherit the Shabbat in love and favor.

A chain of transmission. This inheritance is being transmitted from one generation of Jews to another. Each new generation receives it through and from its parent generation. Each parent generation has a challenge to transmit the inheritance, enhanced and enriched.

Each generation needs to feel that ultimately we are all inheriting and transmitting something that is divine.

One of the great wonders of the world. Generations of Jews have cherished the Shabbat jewel. They polished it and transformed it into one of the most amazing and most sparkling multifaceted diamonds of all times — one of the great wonders of the world.

The varied facets of שַׁבָּת. In וְשָׁמְרוּ we have encountered some of the rich facets of שַׁבָּת.

וְשָׁמְרוּ contains significant declarations about Shabbat and about the Jewish people in their relationship with God. The emphasis is on the communal! national! and historic dimensions of שַׁבָּת; on a rededication to the Covenant and a reconsecration of "the seventh day."

The personal dimension — יִשְׂמְחוּ and רְצֵה בִמְנוּחָתֵנוּ add a distinct dimension of their own. They add personal prayers dealing with individual aspirations.

These prayers speak of joy and delight and purity and integrity and rest and a share in Torah.

Addressing God — In the prayer רְצֵה בִמְנוּחָתֵנוּ we plead:

O God, please find favor in our rest and may the people who sanctify Your name rest on it.

We pray: Please, sanctify us with Your commandments and give us a portion in Your Torah.

Do purify our hearts to serve You in truth. Do satisfy us with Your bounty and make us rejoice in Your salvation.

*Source: Talmud, Shabbat 10b.

In the prayer יִשְׂמְחוּ we ask:

May those of us who observe the Shabbat and call it a delight rejoice in Your Kingship. Let them be satisfied and delighted with Your bounty.

Two kinds of Holiness — Our two prayers speak of holiness, indeed of two kinds of holiness.

A. We speak of holiness that flows from God:
   You (God) have favored the seventh day and have sanctified it. Praised be God who sanctifies the Shabbat.
   We plead: Sanctify us by Your Commandments and make us inherit Your Sabbath of holiness.
B. But we also speak of another kind of holiness that flows towards God:
   about the Jewish people who sanctify the seventh day and who sanctify Your (i.e. God's) name.
   By our actions, we have the power to make God's name holy.   What a privilege and what a challenge!.

רְצֵה בִמְנוּחָתֵנוּ and יִשְׂמְחוּ

A. God sanctifies

Line 5	And the seventh day:	5 וְהַשְּׁבִיעִי רָצִיתָ בּוֹ וְקִדַּשְׁתּוֹ
	You have favored it and sanctified it	10 קַדְּשֵׁנוּ בְּמִצְוֹתֶיךָ
line 10	Make us holy with Your commandments	15-16 וְהַנְחִילֵנוּ... שַׁבַּת קָדְשֶׁךָ
line 15,16	Let us inherit Your Shabbat of holiness	18 בָּרוּךְ אַתָּה ה' מְקַדֵּשׁ הַשַּׁבָּת.
line 18	Praised be You, O Lord,	
	who sanctifies the Sabbath	

B. The Jew sanctifies

Line 3	the people who sanctify the seventh day	3 עַם מְקַדְּשֵׁי שְׁבִיעִי
line 17	and may the people of Israel who sanctify your name rest thereon	17 וְיָנוּחוּ בָו יִשְׂרָאֵל מְקַדְּשֵׁי שְׁמֶךָ

Expressions of joy:

line 1	May they rejoice in Your Kingship	1 יִשְׂמְחוּ בְמַלְכוּתְךָ
line 2	Those who call it (Shabbat) a delight	2 קוֹרְאֵי עוֹנֶג
line 4	May they be delighted in Your bounty	4 יִתְעַנְּגוּ מִטּוּבֶךָ
line 6	You called it the most desirable of days	6 חֶמְדַּת יָמִים אוֹתוֹ קָרָאתָ
line 12	Satisfy us with Your bounty	12 שַׂבְּעֵנוּ מִטּוּבֶךָ
line 13	and make us rejoice in Your salvation	13 וְשַׂמְּחֵנוּ בִּישׁוּעָתֶךָ

Rest

line 9	Find favor in our rest	9 רְצֵה בִמְנוּחָתֵנוּ
line 17	And may Israel rest thereon	17 וְיָנוּחוּ בָה יִשְׂרָאֵל

Study, Purity, Integrity

Line 10	Sanctify us with Your commandments	10 קַדְּשֵׁנוּ בְּמִצְוֹתֶיךָ
line 11	and give us a portion in Your Torah	11 וְתֵן חֶלְקֵנוּ בְּתוֹרָתֶךָ
line 14	Purify our hearts	14 וְטַהֵר לִבֵּנוּ
line 14	—to serve You in truth	14 לְעָבְדְּךָ בֶּאֱמֶת.

*See "Vocabulary of Jewish Life" in Part II.

ASHREY — אַשְׁרֵי

Happy is...
Happy are those who dwell in Your house; they will ever praise You.
Happy is the people who is thus favored; happy is the people whose God is the Lord.

אַשְׁרֵי

(in your סִדּוּר on page.....)

A. Happy are those who dwell in Your house; they will ever praise You. אַשְׁרֵי יוֹשְׁבֵי בֵיתֶךָ; עוֹד יְהַלְלוּךָ, סֶלָה.

B. Happy is the people who is thus favored; אַשְׁרֵי הָעָם שֶׁכָּכָה לּוֹ;

Happy is the people whose God is the Lord. אַשְׁרֵי הָעָם שֶׁה' אֱלֹהָיו.

Psalm 145

A hymn of praise by David תְּהִלָּה לְדָוִד

1a. I will extol You, my God the King, אֲרוֹמִמְךָ, אֱלֹהַי הַמֶּלֶךְ, 1a

b. And I will bless Your name forever and ever. וַאֲבָרְכָה שִׁמְךָ לְעוֹלָם וָעֶד. b

2a. Every day I will bless You בְּכָל יוֹם אֲבָרְכֶךָ, 2a

b. And praise Your name forever and ever. וַאֲהַלְלָה שִׁמְךָ לְעוֹלָם וָעֶד. b

3a. Great is the Lord and most worthy of praise; גָּדוֹל ה' וּמְהֻלָּל מְאֹד, 3a

b. There is no end to the probing of His greatness. וְלִגְדֻלָּתוֹ אֵין חֵקֶר. b

4a. One generation shall laud Your works to another דּוֹר לְדוֹר יְשַׁבַּח מַעֲשֶׂיךָ, 4a

b. They shall recount Your mighty acts. וּגְבוּרֹתֶיךָ יַגִּידוּ. b

5a. On the splendor of the glory of Your majesty הֲדַר כְּבוֹד הוֹדֶךָ, 5a

b. And on Your wondrous deeds will I meditate. וְדִבְרֵי נִפְלְאֹתֶיךָ אָשִׂיחָה. b

6a. They shall speak of the might of Your awesome acts וֶעֱזוּז נוֹרְאֹתֶיךָ יֹאמֵרוּ, 6a

b. And I will tell of Your greatness. וּגְדוּלָּתְךָ אֲסַפְּרֶנָּה. b

7a. They shall express the recollections of Your great goodness זֵכֶר רַב טוּבְךָ יַבִּיעוּ, 7a

b. And sing of Your righteousness. וְצִדְקָתְךָ יְרַנֵּנוּ. b

8a. Gracious and merciful is the Lord, חַנּוּן וְרַחוּם ה', 8a

b. Slow to anger and abundant in kindness. אֶרֶךְ אַפַּיִם וּגְדָל חָסֶד. b

9a. The Lord is good to all, טוֹב ה' לַכֹּל, 9a

b. And His mercies (= His compassion) are over all His works. וְרַחֲמָיו עַל כָּל מַעֲשָׂיו. b

10a. All Your works shall thank You, O Lord יוֹדוּךָ ה' כָּל מַעֲשֶׂיךָ, 10a

b. And Your faithful followers (= Your performers of kindness) shall bless You. וַחֲסִידֶיךָ יְבָרְכוּכָה. b

89

11a.	They shall speak of the glory of Your kingship	כְּבוֹד מַלְכוּתְךָ יֹאמֵרוּ 11a
b.	And talk of Your might!	וּגְבוּרָתְךָ יְדַבֵּרוּ. b
12a.	To let the children of mankind know Your (= His) mighty deeds,	לְהוֹדִיעַ לִבְנֵי הָאָדָם גְּבוּרֹתָיו, 12a
b.	And the glory of the splendor of Your (= His) kingdom.	וּכְבוֹד הֲדַר מַלְכוּתוֹ b
13a.	Your kingdom is a kingdom of eternity (= of all eternities)	מַלְכוּתְךָ מַלְכוּת כָּל עֹלָמִים, 13a
b.	And Your dominion is for all generations.	וּמֶמְשַׁלְתְּךָ בְּכָל דּוֹר וָדוֹר. b
14a.	The Lord upholds all who fall	סוֹמֵךְ ה׳ לְכָל הַנֹּפְלִים, 14a
b.	And raises all who are bowed down.	וְזוֹקֵף לְכָל הַכְּפוּפִים. b
15a.	The eyes of all look hopefully to You,	עֵינֵי כֹל אֵלֶיךָ יְשַׂבֵּרוּ 15a
b.	And You give them their food in due season.	וְאַתָּה נוֹתֵן לָהֶם אֶת אָכְלָם בְּעִתּוֹ. b
16a.	You open Your hand	פּוֹתֵחַ אֶת יָדֶךָ 16a
b.	And satisfy every living thing with favor.	וּמַשְׂבִּיעַ לְכָל חַי רָצוֹן. b
17a.	The Lord is righteous in all His ways,	צַדִּיק ה׳ בְּכָל דְּרָכָיו, 17a
b.	And supremely kind in all His deeds.	וְחָסִיד בְּכָל מַעֲשָׂיו. b
18a.	The Lord is near to all who call upon Him	קָרוֹב ה׳ לְכָל קֹרְאָיו, 18a
b.	To all who call upon Him, with sincerity (= truthfulness).	לְכֹל אֲשֶׁר יִקְרָאֻהוּ בֶאֱמֶת. b
19a.	He will fulfill the desire of those who revere Him;	רְצוֹן יְרֵאָיו יַעֲשֶׂה, 19a
b.	He will hear their cry and will save them.	וְאֶת שַׁוְעָתָם יִשְׁמַע וְיוֹשִׁיעֵם. b
20a.	The Lord preserves (= keeps) all who love Him;	שׁוֹמֵר ה׳ אֶת כָּל אֹהֲבָיו, 20a
b.	But all the wicked will He destroy.	וְאֵת כָּל הָרְשָׁעִים יַשְׁמִיד. b
21a.	My mouth shall speak the praise of the Lord;	תְּהִלַּת ה׳ יְדַבֶּר פִּי, 21a
b.	Let all creatures bless His holy name forever and ever.	וִיבָרֵךְ כָּל בָּשָׂר שֵׁם קָדְשׁוֹ לְעוֹלָם וָעֶד. b
22a.	We will bless the Lord from this time forth and forevermore (= unto eternity)	וַאֲנַחְנוּ נְבָרֵךְ יָהּ מֵעַתָּה וְעַד עוֹלָם, 22a
b.	Praise the Lord!	הַלְלוּיָהּ. b

This prayer appears in the following places:

The prayer אַשְׁרֵי occurs twice in the Morning Service.

1) First in שַׁחֲרִית at the beginning of the series of הַלְלוּיָה prayers (p.....)

2) Then at the end of the Torah Service prior to returning the Scroll to the Ark (p.....).

And the third time...

אַשְׁרֵי appears a third time in the Afternoon Service of Mincha (מִנְחָה). It is a major component of the מִנְחָה service (p.....).

The אַשְׁרֵי comes from the Book of Psalms (Psalm 145).

It is a hymn of praise extolling the power of God.

It particularly highlights God's enormous power (and desire) to do good.

Notes.

Each verse contains 2 parallel phrases "a" and "b".

As you read the sequence of the verses you notice an alphabetical acrostic.

One letter in the alphabetical sequence is missing, namely the letter "נון".

Interestingly enough a verse of אַשְׁרֵי beginning with the letter נון was recently discovered among the Dead Sea Scrolls.

"God is near to all who call upon Him . . . He hears their cry and He saves them."

Maurycy Gottlieb. Jews at Prayer on the Day of Atonement. Tel-Aviv Museum.

Comparison and Analysis	New Words	Words with a familiar sound	Words we already know	line
			הָעָם	B
your God אֱלֹהֶיךָ		his God אֱלֹהָיו		B
our God אֱלֹהֵינוּ		my God אֱלֹהַי		1
			the King הַמֶּלֶךְ	1
			forever and ever לְעוֹלָם וָעֶד	1,2,21
			great גָּדוֹל	3
			there is no אֵין	3
לְדוֹר וָדוֹר		דוֹר לְדוֹר		4
glory כָּבוֹד				
			the glory of... כְּבוֹד	5,11,12
			kindness חֶסֶד	8
			good טוֹב	9
			on עַל	9
לְדוֹר וָדוֹר		בְּכָל דוֹר וָדוֹר		13
		in every generation		13
וְאַתָּה = וְ אַתָּה			and you וְאַתָּה	15
hand יָד		your hand יָדְךָ	give נוֹתֵן	15
חַי		כָּל חַי		16
		every living being		
בְּ אֱמֶת			in truth בֶּאֱמֶת	18
			name שֵׁם	21
eternity עוֹלָם		וָעֶד עוֹלָם		22
		and unto eternity		
			all כָּל	

The ideas.

אַשְׁרֵי — Three Times Daily

The threefold repetition of אַשְׁרֵי is not limited to Sabbath Services only. It is part of every Daily Service all year round. The Talmud recommends this threefold repetition as a highly meritorious act.* As a result of 1) this daily repetition, of 2) the frequent recurrence of phrases within the text, and of 3) the acrostic arrangement of the verses, every Jew, even the least learned came to know אַשְׁרֵי by heart.

Hence there emerged a well known Yiddish saying: "he knows the subject as thoroughly as a Jew knows אַשְׁרֵי."

The spirit of goodness

A. The all-permeating spirit of אַשְׁרֵי is the conviction that:

9　The Lord is good to all,
　　and His tender mercies are over all his works

9　טוֹב ה׳ לַכֹּל וְרַחֲמָיו עַל כָּל מַעֲשָׂיו

17　The Lord is righteous in all His ways,
　　and supremely kind in all His works.

17　צַדִּיק ה׳ בְּכָל דְּרָכָיו וְחָסִיד בְּכָל מַעֲשָׂיו

18　The Lord is near unto all who call upon Him,
　　to all who call upon Him in truth.

18　קָרוֹב ה׳ לְכָל קוֹרְאָיו, לְכֹל אֲשֶׁר יִקְרָאוּהוּ בֶאֱמֶת

20　The Lord preserves all that love Him.

20　שׁוֹמֵר ה׳ אֶת כָּל אֹהֲבָיו

B. Above all, God's attributes are: Kindness beyond expectation and helpfulness to those in need.

8　The Lord is gracious and full of compassion,
　　Long forbearing and abundant in kindness.

8　חַנּוּן וְרַחוּם ה׳ אֶרֶךְ אַפַּיִם וּגְדָל חֶסֶד

14　The Lord upholds all who fall
　　and raises up all who are bowed down

14　סוֹמֵךְ ה׳ לְכָל הַנּוֹפְלִים
　　וְזוֹקֵף לְכָל הַכְּפוּפִים

16　You open Your hand
　　and satisfy every living thing with favor.

16　פּוֹתֵחַ אֶת יָדֶךָ וּמַשְׂבִּיעַ לְכָל חַי רָצוֹן.

C. God is good to all,

The most frequently recurring word — 16 times — is כָּל (= all)
a) God is good tl all, not just to some;
b) God is concerned not only with people, but with every living being in nature.

---

*Source: Talmud — *B'rachot 4b.*

The Optimists

The prayerbook, the Psalmist, and the praying Jews are optimistic. They believe in goodness: The theme of God's help and compassion repeats itself throughout the prayerbook.

Besides gratitude the recital of God's deeds of kindness has a secondary effect: to inspire humans to do likewise. "Imitation of God" is conceived by the Talmud as a supreme religious duty. ("As He is merciful, so you be merciful," etc).*

Through the power of suggestion, אַשְׁרֵי has become a constant guide for the pursuit of love and justice.

"The spirit of אַשְׁרֵי "

The "spirit of אַשְׁרֵי " (the themes of optimism, goodness, and helpfulness) permeates the entire prayerbook. Throughout the ages the message of our prayerbook has been the deep ethnic-religious source of our commitment to the ethic of social justice. Though the "real world" may have been cruel, we created a "world of goodness" all around us.

As we rise in the morning (p..... in your prayerbook)

Our awareness of God's supportive role in our lives begins the minute we open our eyes in the morning.

In the early morning blessings (בִּרְכוֹת הַשַׁחַר) ** we declare:

Praised be You, O Lord our God, Master of the Universe

Who opens the eyes of the blind

Clothes the naked

Releases the bound

Raises up them that are bowed down

In the prayer בָּרוּךְ שֶׁאָמַר (p.....)

In the prayer בָּרוּךְ שֶׁאָמַר, which is the opening blessing of פְּסוּקֵי דְזִמְרָא** we extol God who:

...has compassion upon the Earth

...has compassion upon His creatures

...ransoms and delivers.

---

*Source: Talmud, *Shabbat 133b and Sotah 14a.*
**See p. 23 about פְּסוּקֵי דְזִמְרָא and בִּרְכוֹת הַשַׁחַר.

In Psalm 146 (p..... in your prayerbook)

In Psalm 146, which is recited in the Shacharit service right after אַשְׁרֵי God is praised for the following things:
He renders justice to the oppressed
He gives bread to the hungry
The Lord sets the captives free
The Lord opens the eyes of the blind
The Lord raises up them that are bowed down
The Lord loves the righteous
The Lord protects the strangers
He supports (gives courage to) the fatherless and the widow

In the prayer נִשְׁמַת ("The Breath of all the Living") (p.....)

In נִשְׁמַת, which is one of the most beautiful prayer-poems of our tradition, we offer thanks to God for what He does for us each day in a thousand graceful ways:
He is Liberator, Deliverer, Redeemer, and Provider
and a Source of Mercy at every time of trouble and distress
He guides His world in loving-kindness
and His creatures with tender compassion
He arouses those who sleep
and awakens those who slumber
He causes the dumb to speak,
loosenst the bound, supports the falling,
and raises up those that are bowed down.
He delivers the weak from him that is stronger,
the poor and the needy from
those who rob them.

In the prayer עֶזְרַת אֲבוֹתֵינוּ following the שְׁמַע (p.....)

God's image as the Protector of the weak is further amplified
in the blessings following the שְׁמַע in Shacharit .
He humbles the proud and raises up the lowly
He liberates the captives and redeems the meek
He helps the poor
and answers His people when they cry unto Him.

In the עֲמִידָה (p.....)

We sing these words in the Amidah:*
    He sustains the living with lovingkindness
    He supports the falling and heals the ailing
    and sets free those held in bondage.

The message of the Prayerbook

The prayerbook has inspired many generations of parents and children to empathize with:
    the righteous
    the strangers
    the lowly
    the humble
    the poor
    the ailing
    the falling
    the "downtrodden" (= those who are bent down)
    the robbed ones
    the hungry
    the blind
    the dumb
    and the captives.

*See Unit 7 Second Blessing.

PART II

A review of the Aleph-Bet

The consonants.

		אָלֶף	א
בֵית	ב	בֵּית	ב
		גִמֶל	ג
		דָלֶת	ד
		הֵא	ה
		וָו	ו
		זַיִן	ז
		חֵת	ח
		טֵת	ט
		יוּד	י
כַּף כ כָּף ך	כָּף סוֹפִית ד	כָּף	כ
		לַמֶד	ל
	מֵם סוֹפִית ם	מֵם	מ
	נוּן סוֹפִית ן	נוּן	נ
		סַמֶך	ס
		עַיִן	ע
פֵּא פ פֵא	פֵּא סוֹפִית ף	פֵּא	פ
	צַדִי סוֹפִית ץ	צַדִי	צ
		קוּף	ק
		רֵיש	ר
שִׂין ש שִׁין ש		שִׁין	ש
		תָו ת תָו	ת

Consonants which look alike or sound alike.

		א	ע	ה
ו	ב	בּ	ב	ב
			ג	נ
			ד	ר
			ה	ח
			ו	ב
			ח	כ
			ט	ת	ת
ח	ך	כ	כ	ק	ק	כ
		ם	מ	מ	מ	ם
	ן	ג	נ	נ
	ש	ס	ס	ם	ס
			ה	א	ע
		ף	פ	פ	פ
			ץ	צ
			כ	ק
			ר	ד
ס	ש	שׂ	שׁ	שׁ	ס
		ט	ת	ת

The vowels.

- ָ
- י ֵ
- י ִ
- וּ ֹ
- וֹ
- וֹ ו

One Hundred Words
in order of appearance
(A Cross-Reference Chart)

		UNITS
אֵין		1, 2, 3, 12
אֱלֹהֵינוּ	אֱלֹהַי, אֱלֹהָיו, אֱלֹהֶיךָ, הָאֱלֹהִים אֱלֹהֵי, אֱלֹהֵיכֶם, לֵאלֹהִים, אֱלֹהִים	1, 2, 5, 6, 7, 8, 9, 9, 9, 9, 9, 10, 11, 11, 11, 12, 12
אֲדוֹנֵינוּ	(ה׳ =) אֲדֹנָי, אָדוֹן	1, 2, 2, 3, 3, 4, 4, 4, 6, 6, 7, 7, 7, 8, 8, 9, 9, 10, 10, 11, 11
מַלְכֵּנוּ	מֶלֶךְ מַלְכֵי הַמְּלָכִים, מֶלֶךְ, הַמֶּלֶךְ	1, 2, 2, 3, 5, 7, 7, 8, 9, 10, 12
מוֹשִׁיעֵנוּ		1, 9
מִי	וּמִי	1, 7, 7
נוֹדֶה		1
בָּרוּךְ		1, 2, 3, 4, 5, 6, 7, 7, 7, 8, 9, 9, 10, 12
אַתָּה		1, 3, 5, 7, 7, 7, 7, 7, 7, 7, 7, 10, 11, 11
הוּא		1, 2, 3, 3, 3, 3, 3, 3, 9, 9, 9
כְּ	כָ ,כֶ, כְ, כַּ ,כֶּ, כְ	1, 1, 1, 1, 1, 1, 1, 2, 3, 9
לְ	לֵ, לִ, לַ	1, 1, 1, 3, 5, 8, 12
הָעוֹלָם		1, 3, 3, 5, 8, 9, 10
עָלֵינוּ		2, 3, 8
הַכֹּל	כְּכָל, בְּכָל, וּבְכָל, כָּל	2, 2, 2, 3, 3, 3, 6, 6, 7, 7, 9, 9, 9, 12, 12, 12, 12, 12, 12, 12, 12, 12, 12, 12, 12, 12, 12, 12, 12
לֹא		2, 2, 2
הַקָּדוֹשׁ	קְדוֹשִׁים, קָדוֹשׁ	2, 7, 7, 7, 7, 7, 8, 8, 8, 9, 9, 9
בַּשָׁמַיִם	הַשָׁמַיִם	2, 10
הָאָרֶץ		2, 8, 9, 10
עַל		2, 2, 6, 6, 6, 12
הַ	ה	2, 2, 2, 3, 4, 5, 5, 5, 6, 7, 8, 11, 11
בְּ	בֵּ, בִּ, בָּ	2, 2, 3, 6, 6, 7, 8, 9, 10, 11, 11
וְ	וֵ, וָ, וּ	2, 3, 3, 3, 3, 3, 3, 3, 3, 3, 3, 3, 6, 7, 7, 7, 9, 9, 10, 11, 12, 12, 12

VOCABULARY OF JEWISH LIFE

You know more Hebrew than you think. You are using many Hebrew words in your English conversation without being aware of it. Most of these words require no translation when one Jew speaks to another Jew. They do require translation, of course, when speaking to a non-Jew.

In the list below, put two checks next to the word if you know both the word and its meaning (vv). Put one check, if you know the word but are not sure of its full meaning (v). If you know neither the word nor its meaning, leave it without a check. After you become thoroughly familiar with the word and its meaning, check it twice. This will help you measure both your prior knowledge and your progress.

Unit 1

אָמֵן — Amen; expression of consent

Unit 2

סִדוּר — prayerbook

רֹאשׁ הַשָּׁנָה — Head of the Year; New Year

שַׁחֲרִית — Early morning service

מוּסָף — Late morning service; additional service on Shabbat (and holidays)

בְּרָכוֹת — Blessings

פְּסוּקֵי דְזִמְרָא — Chapters (verses) of song

שְׁמַע — "Hear!"; beginning word of "Hear O Israel the Lord our God the Lord is One"

aramaic

עֲמִידָה — Standing Prayer

הוֹצָאַת הַתּוֹרָה — Taking out the Torah

קְרִיאַת הַתּוֹרָה — Reading from the Torah Scroll

הַכְנָסַת הַתּוֹרָה — Returning the Torah Scroll to the Ark

of the

Unit 3

יִשְׂרָאֵל — Israel; Israelite

שָׁלוֹם — Peace

בְּרָכָה — Blessing

תּוֹרָה — Torah; Jewish Holy Scriptures

חַי — Alive

לְחַיִּים — To life!

צְדָקָה — Charity; righteousness

רַחֲמָנוּת — Compassion

אֵל מָלֵא רַחֲמִים — "God full of compassion". (name of Memorial Prayer)

תַּלְמוּד — Post biblical compendium of discussions of Jewish Law, in 63 treatises.

מִדְרָשׁ — Talmudic interpretation of Biblical texts.

Units 4,5

עֲלִיָּה	Going up to the Torah; the honor as well as the portion itself
Troppe	Musical signs by which the Torah text is chanted
בְּרֵאשִׁית	Genesis
שְׁמוֹת	Exodus
וַיִּקְרָא	Leviticus
בְּמִדְבַּר	Numbers
דְּבָרִים	Deuteronomy
חוּמָשׁ	Pentateuch (from Greek); Five Books of Moses
מֹשֶׁה	Moses
צִיּוֹן	Zion
יְרוּשָׁלַיִם	Jerusalem
סֵפֶר תּוֹרָה	Torah Scroll (lit. Book of the Torah)
סוֹפֵר	Scribe (who writes the Torah, T'fillin and M'zuzah)
בַּעַל קְרִיאָה	Torah Reader
עֵץ חַיִּים	Tree of Life; wooden rollers of Torah Scroll.
יָד	Torah pointer (lit. "Hand")
הַגְבָּהָה	Lifting (of Torah)
גְּלִילָה	Rolling (of Torah)
אֲרוֹן הַקֹּדֶשׁ	Holy Ark
(אֲרוֹן קֹדֶשׁ	in Yiddish)
בִּימָה	pulpit; platform from which Torah is read

טַלִּית	Prayer Shawl
צִיצִית	Fringes (of Talit)
פָּרָשָׁה=	Weekly portion (of
סְדְרָה=	Torah reading)
כֹּהֵן	Kohen; Priest; person of priestly descent
לֵוִי	Levite (of the Tribe of Levi); descendant of the priestly assistants of the ancient Temple
יִשְׂרָאֵל	Israelite; Israelite at large (non,Kohen and non,Levite)
שְׁלִישִׁי	Third Aliyah
רְבִיעִי	Fourth Aliyah
חֲמִישִׁי	Fifth Aliyah
שִׁשִּׁי	Sixth Aliyah
שְׁבִיעִי	Seventh Aliyah
הוֹסָפָה	Additional Aliyah
אַחֲרוֹן	Last Aliyah
מַפְטִיר	The "concluder"; the final concluding Aliyah
הַפְטָרָה	portion from the Prophets

Unit 6

קְרִיאַת שְׁמַע	Reciting of the Sh'ma
מְזוּזָה	M'zuzah; parchment scroll on doorpost inscribed with the Sh'ma. ("M'zuzah" is used "as is" without translation.)
תְּפִילִין	phylacteries — worn during prayers, on a weekday morning
תְּפִילִין שֶׁל יַד	T'fillin of the hand (arm)
תְּפִילִין שֶׁל רֹאשׁ	T'fillin of the head
טַלִית קָטָן	"small Talit" (special garment with Tzitzit, worn all day).
אַרְבַּע כַּנְפוֹת	"Four Corners" — small Talit
מִצְוָה	a divine commandment
מִצְוֹת (מִצְווֹת)	divine commandments

105

Unit 7

שְׁמוֹנֶה עֶשְׂרֵה — Eighteen Benedictions;
עֲמִידָה — Standing Prayer; Amidah
אָבוֹת — "Fathers" — name of first Blessing of the Amidah

חַזָּן — Cantor
מִנְיָן — Minyan; quorum of ten required for holding a public service ("Minyan" is used as is, never in translated form)
אַבְרָהָם — Abraham; our first ancestor
יִצְחָק — Isaac; our second ancestor
יַעֲקֹב — Jacob; our third ancestor
מָגֵן דָוִד — Magen David; shield of David; Star of David

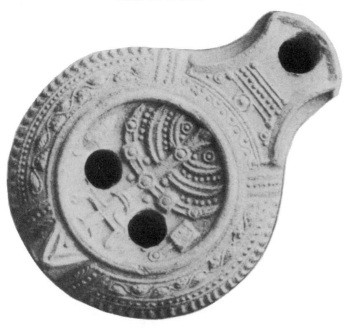

Units 8,9

קְדוּשָׁה — K'dushah; Sanctification of God's name (during the Amidah)
כָּבוֹד — glory; honor
דָוִד — David
מָשִׁיחַ — Messiah; the Anointed One
הַלְלוּיָה — Praise ye the Lord
עַם יִשְׂרָאֵל חַי — The Jewish people lives

Unit 10

שַׁבָּת — Sabbath; day of cessation from work; day of rest.
שׁוֹמֵר שַׁבָּת — A keeper of the Shabbat; a Shabbat observer.
קִדוּשׁ שַׁבָּת — Sanctification of the (or holiday).
בְּרִית — covenant
בְּרִית מִילָה — covenant of circumcision
בּוֹרֵא פְּרִי הַגָפֶן — Who creates the fruit of the wine; Formula of blessing over the wine.
הַמוֹצִיא לֶחֶם מִן הָאָרֶץ — Who brings forth bread from the soil; formula of blessing over bread.

Unit 11

שִׂמְחָה — joy; rejoicing; a happy event
עוֹנֶג — Delight
עוֹנֶג שַׁבָּת — Delight of Shabbat; socializing (and refreshments) in honor of Shabbat in contemporary synagogues.

Unit 12

צַדִּיק   a supremely righteous being

חָסִיד   1) Original meaning: a
supremely kind and virtuous
being (human or divine).
2) Latter meaning: a very
pious person.
3) Contemporary meaning:
a member of the Hassidic
sect. A believer in
Hassidic philosophy and
way of life.

Note on Kaddish

שִׁבְעָה   Seven; "Shiva";
period of seven days of
mourning (used as is,
without translation)

Yahrzeit   "Time of the Year";
(from Yiddish)   the anniversary
date of a death.

קַדִּישׁ   Kaddish; Sanctification.
(this word is never used in
its translated form, but is
used as is).

107

EXERCISES FOR READING FLUENCY (pp......)

Because Hebrew is written phonetically it is easier to read Hebrew than most other languages. Yet when certain sounds of Hebrew like קכּכךּחההבבוׁשׂשּׁסתּתזצ converge upon one another, or two successive Sh'vas occur in the same word, many a reader may be slowed down.

Words containing such sounds were culled from units 1-12 and brought together in the following pages. A frequent and careful rereading of these pages should prove very helpful in developing overall accuracy and fluency.

Unit 1:

אֵין כֵּאלֹהֵינוּ

כֵּאלֹהֵינוּ כַּאדוֹנֵינוּ כְּמַלְכֵּנוּ כְּמוֹשִׁיעֵנוּ

כֵּאלֹהֵינוּ כַּאדוֹנֵינוּ כְּמַלְכֵּנוּ כְּמוֹשִׁיעֵנוּ

Unit 2:

עָלֵינוּ

לְשַׁבֵּחַ כְּגוֹיֵי הָאֲרָצוֹת כְּמִשְׁפְּחוֹת כְּכָל

וַאֲנַחְנוּ כּוֹרְעִים וּמִשְׁתַּחֲוִים .

בַּיּוֹם הַהוּא יִהְיֶה ה' אֶחָד וּשְׁמוֹ אֶחָד .

Unit 3:

אֲדוֹן עוֹלָם

לְעֵת נַעֲשָׂה בְחֶפְצוֹ כֹּל . וְאַחֲרֵי כִּכְלוֹת הַכֹּל .

וְהוּא הָיָה וְהוּא הֹוֶה וְהוּא יִהְיֶה .

לְהַמְשִׁיל לוֹ לְהַחְבִּירָה.

בְּלִי רֵאשִׁית, בְּלִי תַכְלִית.וְעִם רוּחִי גְוִיָתִי.

108

Unit 3:
שִׂים שָׁלוֹם

טוֹבָה וּבְרָכָה בָּעוֹלָם. חֵן וָחֶסֶד וְרַחֲמִים.

בָּרְכֵנוּ אָבִינוּ כֻּלָּנוּ כְּאֶחָד בְּאוֹר פָּנֶיךָ .

תּוֹרַת חַיִּים וְאַהֲבַת חֶסֶד וּצְדָקָה וּבְרָכָה וְרַחֲמִים וְחַיִּים.

וְטוֹב בְּעֵינֶיךָ לְבָרֵךְ אֶת עַמְּךָ יִשְׂרָאֵל בִּשְׁלוֹמֶךָ ·

Unit 4:
הוֹצָאַת הַתּוֹרָה

וַיְהִי בִּנְסֹעַ הָאָרֹן   וַיֹּאמֶר מֹשֶׁה.

קוּמָה ה׳ וְיָפֻצוּ אוֹיְבֶיךָ וְיָנֻסוּ מְשַׂנְאֶיךָ מִפָּנֶיךָ .
הַכְנָסַת הַתּוֹרָה

עֵץ חַיִּים הִיא לַמַּחֲזִיקִים בָּהּ וְתוֹמְכֶיהָ מְאֻשָּׁר.

דְּרָכֶיהָ דַרְכֵי נֹעַם וְכָל נְתִיבוֹתֶיהָ

Unit 5:
בִּרְכוֹת הַתּוֹרָה.

בָּרְכוּ אֶת ה׳ הַמְבוֹרָךְ. בָּרוּךְ ה׳ הַמְבוֹרָךְ.

בָּחַר בָּנוּ מִכָּל הָעַמִּים. וְחַיֵּי עוֹלָם נָטַע בְּתוֹכֵנוּ.

Unit 6:
שְׁמַע

בָּרוּךְ שֵׁם כְּבוֹד מַלְכוּתוֹ.

בְּכָל לְבָבְךָ לְבָנֶיךָ בְּשִׁבְתְּךָ בְּבֵיתֶךָ

וּבְלֶכְתְּךָ בַדֶּרֶךְ וּבְשָׁכְבְּךָ וּבְקוּמֶךָ ·

וּקְשַׁרְתָּם וּכְתַבְתָּם יָדֶךָ עֵינֶיךָ בֵּיתֶךָ וּבִשְׁעָרֶיךָ

Unit 7:

עֲמִידָה

וְזוֹכֵר חַסְדֵי אָבוֹת וּמֵבִיא... לִבְנֵי בְנֵיהֶם... בְּאַהֲבָה

מְכַלְכֵּל חַיִּים בְּחֶסֶד. מֶלֶךְ מֵמִית וּמְחַיֶּה וּמַצְמִיחַ יְשׁוּעָה.

Units 8,9

קְדוּשָׁה

נְקַדֵּשׁ אֶת שִׁמְךָ... כְּשֵׁם שֶׁמַּקְדִּישִׁים אוֹתוֹ בִּשְׁמֵי מָרוֹם .

ה׳ צְבָאוֹת — מְלֹא כָל הָאָרֶץ כְּבוֹדוֹ.

בָּרוּךְ כְּבוֹד ה׳ — מִמְּקוֹמוֹ .

מִמְּקוֹמְךָ... כִּי מְחַכִּים אֲנַחְנוּ לָךְ.

קְדֻשָּׁתְךָ נַקְדִּישׁ, וְשִׁבְחֲךָ .. לֹא יָמוּשׁ

נַעֲרִיצְךָ וְנַקְדִּישְׁךָ כְּסוֹד שִׂיחַ שַׂרְפֵי קֹדֶשׁ ,

הַמַּקְדִּישִׁים שִׁמְךָ.

Unit 10

וְשָׁמְרוּ

וְשָׁמְרוּ בְנֵי יִשְׂרָאֵל אֶת הַשַּׁבָּת לַעֲשׂוֹת אֶת הַשַּׁבָּת

כִּי שֵׁשֶׁת יָמִים עָשָׂה ה׳ אֶת הַשָּׁמַיִם

קָדוֹשׁ

עַל כֵּן בֵּרַךְ. וַיְקַדְּשֵׁהוּ.

Unit 11:

יִשְׂמְחוּ   רְצֵה בִמְנוּחָתֵנוּ

יִשְׂמְחוּ בְמַלְכוּתְךָ שׁוֹמְרֵי שַׁבָּת. עַם מְקַדְּשֵׁי שְׁבִיעִי. וְהַשְּׁבִיעִי רָצִיתָ בּוֹ.

וְשַׂמְּחֵנוּ בִישׁוּעָתֶךָ. יִשְׂרָאֵל מְקַדְּשֵׁי שְׁמֶךָ. מְקַדֵּשׁ הַשַּׁבָּת.

The recurrent phrases

HAPPY IS... אַשְׁרֵי

A	אַשְׁרֵי יוֹשְׁבֵי בֵיתֶךָ
B	אַשְׁרֵי הָעָם שֶׁכָּכָה לּוֹ
B	אַשְׁרֵי הָעָם שֶׁכָּכָה לּוֹ
B	אַשְׁרֵי הָעָם שֶׁה' אֱלֹהָיו

FOREVER AND EVER לְעוֹלָם וָעֶד

1	וַאֲבָרְכָה שִׁמְךָ לְעוֹלָם וָעֶד
2	וַאֲהַלְלָה שִׁמְךָ לְעוֹלָם וָעֶד
21	וִיבָרֵךְ כָּל בָּשָׂר שֵׁם קָדְשׁוֹ לְעוֹלָם וָעֶד

WE'LL BLESS נְבָרֵךְ

1	וַאֲבָרְכָה שִׁמְךָ לְעוֹלָם וָעֶד
2	בְּכָל יוֹם אֲבָרְכֶךָ
10	וַחֲסִידֶיךָ יְבָרְכוּכָה
21	וִיבָרֵךְ כָּל בָּשָׂר שֵׁם קָדְשׁוֹ
22	וַאֲנַחְנוּ נְבָרֵךְ יָהּ

PRAISE YE THE LORD הַלְלוּיָהּ

A	עוֹד יְהַלְלוּךָ סֶלָה
3	גָּדוֹל ה' וּמְהֻלָּל מְאֹד
22	הַלְלוּיָהּ

NAME שֵׁם

1	וַאֲבָרְכָה שִׁמְךָ לְעוֹלָם וָעֶד
2	וַאֲהַלְלָה שִׁמְךָ לְעוֹלָם וָעֶד
2	וַאֲהַלְלָה שִׁמְךָ לְעוֹלָם וָעֶד
21	וִיבָרֵךְ כָּל בָּשָׂר שֵׁם קָדְשׁוֹ לְעוֹלָם וָעֶד

YOUR WORKS מַעֲשֶׂיךָ

4	דּוֹר לְדוֹר יְשַׁבַּח מַעֲשֶׂיךָ
9	וְרַחֲמָיו עַל כָּל מַעֲשָׂיו
17	וְחָסִיד בְּכָל מַעֲשָׂיו
10	יוֹדוּךָ ה' כָּל מַעֲשֶׂיךָ

YOUR MIGHTY DEEDS גְּבוּרוֹתֶיךָ

4	וּגְבוּרוֹתֶיךָ יַגִּידוּ
11	וּגְבוּרָתְךָ יְדַבֵּרוּ
12	לְהוֹדִיעַ לִבְנֵי הָאָדָם גְּבוּרוֹתָיו

GENERATION TO GENERATION דּוֹר לְדוֹר

4	דּוֹר לְדוֹר יְשַׁבַּח מַעֲשֶׂיךָ
13	וּמֶמְשַׁלְתְּךָ בְּכָל דּוֹר וָדוֹר

TWO HYMNS FOR PRACTICE

We recommend the two hymns below as excellent exercises for reading fluency. Try to practice them with your congregational tune. Your cantor's cassette (see introduction to this book) should include these hymns.

From the שַׁחֲרִית Service
(p..... in your סִדּוּר)

אֵל אָדוֹן עַל כָּל־הַמַּעֲשִׂים	בָּרוּךְ וּמְבֹרָךְ בְּפִי כָּל־נְשָׁמָה׃
גָּדְלוֹ וְטוּבוֹ מָלֵא עוֹלָם	דַּעַת וּתְבוּנָה סֹבְבִים אֹתוֹ׃
הַמִּתְגָּאֶה עַל חַיּוֹת הַקֹּדֶשׁ	וְנֶהְדָּר בְּכָבוֹד עַל־הַמֶּרְכָּבָה׃
זְכוּת וּמִישׁוֹר לִפְנֵי כִסְאוֹ	חֶסֶד וְרַחֲמִים לִפְנֵי כְבוֹדוֹ׃
טוֹבִים מְאוֹרוֹת שֶׁבָּרָא אֱלֹהֵינוּ	יְצָרָם בְּדַעַת בְּבִינָה וּבְהַשְׂכֵּל׃
כֹּחַ וּגְבוּרָה נָתַן בָּהֶם	לִהְיוֹת מוֹשְׁלִים בְּקֶרֶב תֵּבֵל׃
מְלֵאִים זִיו וּמְפִיקִים נֹגַהּ	נָאֶה זִיוָם בְּכָל־הָעוֹלָם׃
שְׂמֵחִים בְּצֵאתָם וְשָׂשִׂים בְּבֹאָם	עֹשִׂים בְּאֵימָה רְצוֹן קוֹנָם׃
פְּאֵר וְכָבוֹד נוֹתְנִים לִשְׁמוֹ	צָהֳלָה וְרִנָּה לְזֵכֶר מַלְכוּתוֹ׃
קָרָא לַשֶּׁמֶשׁ וַיִּזְרַח אוֹר	רָאָה וְהִתְקִין צוּרַת הַלְּבָנָה׃

שֶׁבַח נוֹתְנִים לוֹ כָּל־צְבָא מָרוֹם

תִּפְאֶרֶת וּגְדֻלָּה שְׂרָפִים וְאוֹפַנִּים וְחַיּוֹת הַקֹּדֶשׁ

מִזְמוֹר לְדָוִד

הָבוּ לַיהוָה בְּנֵי אֵלִים   הָבוּ לַיהוָה כָּבוֹד וָעֹז:

הָבוּ לַיהוָה כְּבוֹד שְׁמוֹ   הִשְׁתַּחֲווּ לַיהוָה בְּהַדְרַת־
קֹדֶשׁ:

קוֹל יְהוָה עַל־הַמַּיִם   אֵל הַכָּבוֹד הִרְעִים
יְהוָה עַל־מַיִם רַבִּים:

קוֹל יְהוָה בַּכֹּחַ   קוֹל יְהוָה בֶּהָדָר:

קוֹל יְהוָה שֹׁבֵר אֲרָזִים   וַיְשַׁבֵּר יְהוָה אֶת־אַרְזֵי
הַלְּבָנוֹן:

וַיַּרְקִידֵם כְּמוֹ־עֵגֶל   לְבָנוֹן וְשִׂרְיוֹן כְּמוֹ בֶן־
רְאֵמִים:

קוֹל יְהוָה חֹצֵב לַהֲבוֹת אֵשׁ:

קוֹל יְהוָה יָחִיל מִדְבָּר   יָחִיל יְהוָה מִדְבַּר קָדֵשׁ:

קוֹל יְהוָה יְחוֹלֵל אַיָּלוֹת   וַיֶּחֱשֹׂף יְעָרוֹת
וּבְהֵיכָלוֹ כֻּלּוֹ אֹמֵר כָּבוֹד:

יְהוָה לַמַּבּוּל יָשָׁב   וַיֵּשֶׁב יְהוָה מֶלֶךְ לְעוֹלָם:

יְהוָה עֹז לְעַמּוֹ יִתֵּן   יְהוָה יְבָרֵךְ אֶת־עַמּוֹ בַשָּׁלוֹם:

LEARN TO CHANT THE קַדִּישׁ

Not only mourners need to know the קַדִּישׁ.
When the Cantor chants the Reader's Kaddish, the worshippers frequently join in singing with him the parts underlined below.
Please note 3 main varieties of קַדִּישׁ

A. Reader's "half Kaddish"	lines 1-14
B. Reader's "full Kaddish"	lines 1-24
C. Mourners' Kaddish	lines 1-14
	plus lines 19-24
	(lines 15-18 are omitted.)

1. יִתְגַּדַּל וְיִתְקַדַּשׁ שְׁמֵהּ רַבָּא
2. בְּעָלְמָא דִּי בְרָא כִרְעוּתֵהּ
3. וְיַמְלִיךְ מַלְכוּתֵהּ בְּחַיֵּיכוֹן וּבְיוֹמֵיכוֹן
4. <u>וּבְחַיֵּי דְכָל בֵּית יִשְׂרָאֵל</u>
5. <u>בַּעֲגָלָא וּבִזְמַן קָרִיב</u>
6. וְאִמְרוּ אָמֵן.
7. <u>יְהֵא שְׁמֵהּ רַבָּא מְבָרַךְ לְעָלַם וּלְעָלְמֵי עָלְמַיָּא</u>
8. יִתְבָּרַךְ וְיִשְׁתַּבַּח, וְיִתְפָּאַר וְיִתְרוֹמַם
9. וְיִתְנַשֵּׂא וְיִתְהַדָּר, וְיִתְעַלֶּה וְיִתְהַלָּל
10. שְׁמֵהּ דְּקֻדְשָׁא, בְּרִיךְ הוּא.
11. לְעֵלָּא מִן כָּל בִּרְכָתָא וְשִׁירָתָא
12. <u>תֻּשְׁבְּחָתָא וְנֶחֱמָתָא</u>
13. <u>דַּאֲמִירָן בְּעָלְמָא</u>
14. וְאִמְרוּ אָמֵן.

15. תִּתְקַבֵּל צְלוֹתְהוֹן וּבָעוּתְהוֹן
16. דְּכָל יִשְׂרָאֵל
17. קֳדָם אֲבוּהוֹן דִּי בִשְׁמַיָּא
18. וְאִמְרוּ אָמֵן

19. יְהֵא שְׁלָמָא רַבָּא מִן שְׁמַיָּא וְחַיִּים,
20. עָלֵינוּ וְעַל כָּל יִשְׂרָאֵל
21. וְאִמְרוּ אָמֵן.
22. עֹשֶׂה שָׁלוֹם בִּמְרוֹמָיו
23. <u>הוּא יַעֲשֶׂה שָׁלוֹם עָלֵינוּ וְעַל כָּל יִשְׂרָאֵל</u>
24. וְאִמְרוּ אָמֵן.

A NOTE ON קַדִּישׁ

Originally

Originally Kaddish was not a mourner's prayer.
It was a hymn of praise intended as a conclusion to a public session of religious study or to a section of a worship service. It expresses (a) an exalted glorification of God, (b) an acceptance of God's world, (c) a hope for the establishment of God's Kingship on earth — speedily, in our lifetime, (d) and a yearning for harmony and peace.

How did the Kaddish become a mourner's prayer?

It happened in stages. The Kaddish was usually recited at the conclusion of a study session held at the house of mourners during "Shiva."* In time some families began to omit the study session but the Kaddish remained as a "constant." Eventually people began to identify the Kaddish with mourning rituals.
As a mourners' prayer Kaddish is recited during the first eleven months following a death in the family and on the Yahrzeit, the Hebrew anniversary date of the death.

What is the message of the Kaddish for the mourners?

The message of the קַדִּישׁ is highly optimistic and reassuring about the future. The Mourner's Kaddish has no mention of death. When it is recited in honor of the deceased, its message is for the living. The message is: accept God's world as it is and as God wanted it to be. Rejoin the living (in tribute to the deceased). Hope and pray and work for a world of godliness. The mourner is invited to say "yes" to life, to the world, and to God.

The Reader's Kaddish.

The Reader's Kaddish is part of every Jewish public service. It comes in a number of variations as a divider to separate major sections of the Service. The most frequent ones were mentioned on the previous page.
With the exception of a few Hebrew lines the language of the Kaddish is Aramaic, which was the vernacular spoken by Jews in the days of the Talmud. (In fact the Talmud was also written in Aramaic). Aramaic is a language akin to Hebrew.

---

*"Shiva" (= שִׁבְעָה) — Seven day period of mourning.

Chart of prefixes and suffixes

The definite article, conjunctions, prepositions and pronouns.

הַיּוֹם = the day this day	the; this	הַ =
הָאָרֶץ = the earth	the; this	הָ =
בְּיַד, בַּיּוֹם, בָּעוֹלָם	in; on	בּ = (בְּ בַּ בָּ)
כְּמַלְכֵּנוּ, כַּאֲדוֹנֵינוּ, כֵּאלֹהֵינוּ, כְּמַלְכֵּנוּ, כַּאֲדוֹנֵינוּ,	like	כּ = (כְּ כַּ כֵּ כַ כֶ)
לְמַלְכֵּנוּ, לַאֲדוֹנֵינוּ, לֵאלֹהֵינוּ	to	ל = (לְ לַ לֵ)
מִכָּל	from	מ = (מִ)
וְהוּא וָחֶסֶד וּמִי	and	ו = (וְ וָ וּ)
אֵלִי = my God	mine	...יִ =
עַמְּךָ = your people	yours	...ךָ =
יָדוֹ = his hand	his	...וֹ =
אֱלֹהֵינוּ = our God	our	...נוּ =
אֱלֹהֵיכֶם = your God	your (in the plural)	...כֶם =
קַדְּשֵׁנוּ = make us holy	us (when attached to a verb)	...נוּ =

Some more grammar for the advanced learner

אֲנִי ה׳ אֱלֹהֵיכֶם	I	אֲנִי
בָּרוּךְ אַתָּה	you	אַתָּה
הוּא אֱלֹהֵינוּ	he	הוּא
וַאֲנַחְנוּ כּוֹרְעִים	we	אֲנַחְנוּ
וְנָתַן לָנוּ אֶת תּוֹרָתוֹ; אֲשֶׁר בָּחַר בָּנוּ	בָּנוּ = בָּ נוּ	לָנוּ = לָ נוּ
עָלֵינוּ לְשַׁבֵּחַ	Upon us = עָלֵינוּ	עַל on ; upon
אֲדוֹן עוֹלָם אֲשֶׁר מָלַךְ	who	אֲשֶׁר
הַדְּבָרִים הָאֵלֶּה אֲשֶׁר אָנֹכִי מְצַוְּךָ	which	אֲשֶׁר
שֶׁלֹּא עָשָׂנוּ כְּגוֹיֵי הָאֲרָצוֹת	that	...שֶׁ = אֲשֶׁר
אֲרוֹמִמְךָ, אֱלֹהַי הַמֶּלֶךְ	my God	אֱלֹהַי
וְאָהַבְתָּ אֵת ה׳ אֱלֹהֶיךָ	your God (when talking to a male)	אֱלֹהֶיךָ
אֱלֹהַיִךְ צִיּוֹן	your God (when talking to a female)	אֱלֹהַיִךְ
אַשְׁרֵי הָעָם שֶׁה׳ אֱלֹהָיו	his God	אֱלֹהָיו
בָּרוּךְ אֱלֹהֵינוּ	our God	אֱלֹהֵינוּ
אֲנִי ה׳ אֱלֹהֵיכֶם	your God (when talking to many)	אֱלֹהֵיכֶם
אֱלֹהֵי אַבְרָהָם	the God of ...	אֱלֹהֵי

EXTENDED HEBREW VOCABULARLY
For the advanced

Comparison and Analysis		New Words		Words with a familiar ring		Words we already know		Unit 2
beginning	רֵאשִׁית	In the beginning	בְּרֵאשִׁית					1
that	שֶׁ	that...not	שֶׁלֹּא					2a,3a
	שֶׁ לֹא							
and	וְ	and...not	וְלֹא					2b
on	עַל		וְעַל					10
	וְ עַל							
		he shall be	יִהְיֶה					18
name	שֵׁם	his name	שְׁמוֹ					18
						אֲדוֹן עוֹלָם		
		who (in a statement) not in a question	אֲשֶׁר					1
king	מֶלֶךְ	reigned	מָלַךְ					1
						King	מֶלֶךְ	2
Name	שֵׁם					his name	שְׁמוֹ	
	מֶלֶךְ	he will reign	יִמְלוֹךְ					3
						he shall be	יִהְיֶה	4
in the beginning	בְּ רֵאשִׁית			beginning	רֵאשִׁית			6
	וְ לֹא					and...not	וְלֹא	10

119

Comparison and Analysis	New Words	Words with a familiar ring	Words we already know	שִׂים שָׁלוֹם
וְ עַל			and on · וְעַל	3
people · עַם (עַם יִשְׂרָאֵל חַי)		your people · עַמְּךָ		3
בָּרוּךְ · בָּרֵךְ נוּ		bless us · בָּרְכֵנוּ		4
כָּל כֻּלָּ נוּ		all of us · כֻּלָּנוּ		4
		you gave · נָתַתָּ		6
לָנוּ = לָ נוּ		to us · לָנוּ		6
בָּרוּךְ לְ בָרֵךְ		to bless · לְבָרֵךְ		10
בְּכָל = בְּ כָל		in all; at all · בְּכָל		11
וּבְכָל = וּ בְ כָל		and in all · וּבְכָל		11
שָׁלוֹם בְּ שְׁלוֹמֶ ךָ		with your peace · בִּשְׁלוֹמֶךָ		11
בָּרוּךְ		who blesses · הַמְבָרֵךְ		13
people · עַם		his people · עַמּוֹ		13
עַמּוֹ = עַמּ וֹ				
				Unit 5
Word · דָּבָר	The word of God · דְּבַר ה׳		who; which · אֲשֶׁר	
gave · נָתַן		who gave · שֶׁנָּתַן		
לְעַמּוֹ = לְ עַמּוֹ (עַם)		to his people · לְעַמּוֹ		
way · דֶּרֶךְ	her ways · דְּרָכֶיהָ			
way · דֶּרֶךְ	the ways of.. · דַּרְכֵי			

120

Comparison and Analysis	New Words	Words with a familiar ring	Words we already know	Unit 5
בָּרוּךְ		Bless, (Praise!) בָּרְכוּ		AAI
בָּרוּךְ		who is to be praised הַמְבוֹרָךְ		AAI
			who (in a statement) אֲשֶׁר	A2, B2
מִכָּל = מִ כָּל		from all מִכָּל		A2
לָנוּ = לָ נוּ			to us; (to) us לָנוּ	A3,B2
You gave נָתַתָּ		he gave נָתַן		A3,B2
he gives נוֹתֵן				
חַי חַיִּים לְחַיִּים		and life of... וְחַיֵּי		B3
בָּנוּ = בָּ נוּ		in us; (in) us בָּנוּ		A2
				Unit 6
King מֶלֶךְ		his Kingship מַלְכוּתוֹ		2
soul נֶפֶשׁ	your soul נַפְשְׁךָ			4
נַפְשְׁ ךָ				
heart לֵב	your heart לְבָבְךָ			4,6
לְבָבְךָ				
			which אֲשֶׁר	6
בָּנֶי ךָ	to your sons לְבָנֶיךָ			7
house בַּיִת	in your house בְּבֵיתֶךָ			9
כְּ בֵיתֶךָ				
sign אוֹת	for a sign לְאוֹת			12
to; for לְ				
לְאוֹת = לְ אוֹת				
house בַּיִת	your house בֵּיתֶךָ			15
בֵּיתֶךָ				

Comparison and Analysis	New Words	Words with a familiar ring	Words we already know	Unit 7
kindness חֶסֶד	gestows גּוֹמֵל חֲסָדִים			5
גְּמִילוּת חֶסֶד	kindnesses חֲסָדִים			
(An act of kindness				5
e.g. a free loan)		kindnesses of... חַסְדֵי		7
ל כְּנֵי בְּנֵי הֶם		to their children's children לִכְנֵי בְנֵיהֶם		8
בְּנֵי יִשְׂרָאֵל				
name שֵׁם			his name שְׁמוֹ	9
	in love בְּאַהֲבָה			
our Deliverer מוֹשִׁיעֵנוּ		and Deliverer וּמוֹשִׁיעַ		10
וּמוֹשִׁיעַ = וּ מוֹשִׁיעַ				
				גְּבוּרוֹת
life חַיִּים		revives; bestows life מְחַיֶּה		2,6,16
מוֹשִׁיעֵנוּ מוֹשִׁיעַ		to deliver לְהוֹשִׁיעַ		3
	he supports סוֹמֵךְ			7
	the falling נוֹפְלִים			7
	mighty deeds גְּבוּרוֹת			11
alive; is alive חַי	who revives; who bestows life מְחַיֶּה			13
Deliverer מוֹשִׁיעַ	deliverance יְשׁוּעָה			13
	to revive; to bestow life. לְהַחֲיוֹת			14
				קְדוּשַׁת הַשֵּׁם
his name שְׁמוֹ		and your name וְשִׁמְךָ		2
וְשִׁמְךָ = וּ שִׁמְךָ				
Praise the Lord הַלְלוּיָה	they will praise you יְהַלְלוּךְ			4

122

Comparison and Analysis		New Words	Words with a familiar ring		Words we already know		Unit 8
from his place	מִמְּקוֹמוֹ מִמְּקוֹמְךָ		from your place	מִמְּקוֹמְךָ			12
he will reign	יִמְלוֹךְ		and you shall reign	וְתִמְלוֹךְ			13
	יִמְלוֹךְ		you shall reign	תִּמְלוֹךְ			14
your eyes	עֵינֶיךָ		and our eyes	וְעֵינֵינוּ			22
וְעֵינֵינוּ = וְ עֵינֵי נוּ			your				22
his Kingship	מַלְכוּתוֹ		Kingship	מַלְכוּתֶךָ			
King	מֶלֶךְ				he will reign	יִמְלוֹךְ	24
							Unit 9
one	אֶחָד		who proclaims the unity	הַמְיַחֲדִים			13
name	שֵׁם				his name	שְׁמוֹ	13
Eternal light	נֵר תָּמִיד		perpetually	תָּמִיד			14
					in love	בְּאַהֲבָה	15
hear	שְׁמַע		may he make us hear	יַשְׁמִיעֵנוּ			19
mercy	רַחֲמִים		in his mercy	בְּרַחֲמָיו			19
לְעֵינֵי = לְ עֵינֵי עֵינֵינוּ			before the eyes	לְעֵינֵי			20
King	מֶלֶךְ				he shall reign	יִמְלוֹךְ	24

123

Comparison and Analysis	New Words	Words with a familiar ring	Words we already know	Unit 10
שׁוֹמֵר שַׁבָּת keeper of the Shabbat	and they shall keep וְשָׁמְרוּ			1
	to make לַעֲשׂוֹת			2
from generation to generation לְדוֹר וָדוֹר		throughout their generations לְדוֹרוֹתָם		3
between בֵּין עֵינֶיךָ your eyes		between בֵּינִי וּבֵין between me and		5
		a sign אוֹת		6
the sixth Aliyah שִׁשִּׁי		six שֵׁשֶׁת		7
day יוֹם		days יָמִים		7
to do לַעֲשׂוֹת		he made עָשָׂה		7
		and on the seventh		7
seventh (Aliyah) שְׁבִיעִי		day וּבַיּוֹם הַשְּׁבִיעִי		8
Shabbat שַׁבָּת		he ceased שָׁבַת from work.		8
	and he was refreshed וַיִּנָּפַשׁ			8

Comparison and Analysis	New Words	Words with a familiar ring	Words we already know	יִשְׂמְחוּ
joy שִׂמְחָה		may they rejoice יִשְׂמְחוּ		1
בְּ מַלְכוּתְךָ		in your Kingship בְּמַלְכוּתְךָ		1
keeper שׁוֹמֵר			keepers of... שׁוֹמְרֵי	2
		those who sanctify מְקַדְּשֵׁי		3
good טוֹב		from your goodness מִטּוּבֶךָ		4
קָדוֹשׁ		and you shall sanctify it וְקִדַּשְׁתּוֹ		5
day יוֹם			days יָמִים	6
			Genesis; בְּרֵאשִׁית	7
delight עוֹנֶג		and they shall be delighted וְיִתְעַנְּגוּ		
				רְצֵה בִמְנוּחָתֵנוּ
rest מְנוּחָה	in our rest בִּמְנוּחָתֵנוּ			9
קָדוֹשׁ		sanctify us קַדְּשֵׁנוּ		9
בְּ מִצְווֹתֶי ךָ		by your commandments בְּמִצְוֺתֶיךָ		10
בְּ תּוֹרָתֶ ךָ		בְּתוֹרָתֶךָ		11
מִ טּוּבְ ךָ		from your goodness מִטּוּבֶךָ		12
שִׂמְחָה יִשְׂמְחוּ		and make us rejoice וְשַׂמְּחֵנוּ		13

Comparison and Analysis	New Words	Words with a familiar ring	Words we already know	Unit 11
לֵבּ נוּ		our heart לִבֵּנוּ		14
לְבָבֶךָ		your holy Sabbath		15
קֹדֶשׁ שַׁבָּת קֹדֶשׁ		שַׁבַּת קָדְשֶׁךָ		16
	and may they			17
rest מְנוּחָה	rest וְיָנוּחוּ			17
who sanctifies מְקַדֵּשׁ			who sanctify מְקַדְּשֵׁי	17
your name שְׁמֶךָ			your name שְׁמֶךָ	17
who sanctify מְקַדְּשֵׁי		מְקַדֵּשׁ		18

				Unit 12
			your house בֵּיתֶךָ	A
			your name שְׁמֶךָ	1,2
			and your mighty deeds וּגְבוּרוֹתֶיךָ	4,11,12
			and His mercies וְרַחֲמָיו	9
			Kingship מַלְכוּת	13
			your Kingship מַלְכוּתְךָ	11,13
			his Kingship מַלְכוּתוֹ	12
			eternities עוֹלָמִים	13
			supports סוֹמֵךְ	14
			the falling נוֹפְלִים	14
			the eyes of... עֵינֵי	15
			who אֲשֶׁר	17
			His holiness קָדְשׁוֹ	21
			and unto eternity וְעַד עוֹלָם	22

126

BASIC JEWISH BIBLIOGRAPHY ON JEWISH PRAYER

SIDDURUM WITH COMMENTARIES

1. Birnbaum, Philip, ed., Daily Prayer Book: Ha-Siddur Hashalem N.Y., 1949 (repr. many times)
2. Hertz, Joseph H., ed., The Authorized Daily Prayer Book, Revised Edition, N.Y., 1946 (repr. many times)

JEWISH PRAYER: HISTORY, MEANING, AND PRACTICE

1. Brown, Steven M. and Garfinkel, Stephen, Higher and Higher: Making Jewish Prayer Part of Us, N.Y., 1979
2. Donin, Hayim, To Pray as a Jew, N.Y., 1980.
3. Arian, Philip and Eisenberg, Azriel, The Story of the Prayer Book, Hartford, 1968
4. Garfiel, Evelyn, The Service of the Heart: A Guide to the Jewish Prayer Book, N.Y., 1958 (reprinted in pb.)
5. Idelsohn, A.Z., Jewish Liturgy and Its Development, N.Y., 1932 (reprinted in pb.)
6. Jacobson, B.S., The Weekday Siddur: An Exposition and Analysis of its Structure, Contents, Language, and Ideas, Tel Aviv, 1973
7. Millgram, Abraham, Jewish Worship, Philadephia, 1971
8. Munk, Elie, The World of Prayer, N.Y., 1961 (repr. in pb.)

THE PHILOSOPHY AND IDEAS OF JEWISH PRAYER

1. Heschel, A.J., Man's Quest for God: Studies in Prayer and Symbolism, N.Y., 1954
2. Jacobs, Louis, Jewish Prayer, London, 1955 (repr. twice)
3. Jacobson, B.S., Meditations on the Siddur: Studies in the Essential Problems and Ideas of Jewish Worship, Tel Aviv, 1966
4. Petuchowski, Jakob J. Understanding Jewish Prayer, N.Y., 1972